First World War
and Army of Occupation
War Diary
France, Belgium and Germany

38 DIVISION
Divisional Troops
77 Sanitary Section
4 December 1915 - 30 April 1917

WO95/2550/3

The Naval & Military Press Ltd
www.nmarchive.com
Published in association with The National Archives

Published by

The Naval & Military Press Ltd

Unit 10 Ridgewood Industrial Park,

Uckfield, East Sussex,

TN22 5QE England

Tel: +44 (0) 1825 749494

www.naval-military-press.com

www.nmarchive.com

This diary has been reprinted in facsimile from the original. Any imperfections are inevitably reproduced and the quality may fall short of modern type and cartographic standards.

© **Crown Copyright**
Images reproduced by permission of The National Archives, London, England, 2015.

Contents

Document type	Place/Title	Date From	Date To
Miscellaneous	WO95/2550/3 77 Sanitary Section		
Heading	38th Division Medical 77th Sanitary Section Dec 1915-1917 Apl		
Heading	38th Div San: Sect. No-77 Vol I December 1915 Dec 16		
War Diary	Southampton	04/12/1915	05/12/1915
War Diary	Havre	06/12/1915	06/12/1915
War Diary	Aire	07/12/1915	07/12/1915
War Diary	Roquetoire	08/12/1915	18/12/1915
War Diary	St Venant	19/12/1915	31/12/1915
Heading	38th Div Jan 1916 San: Sect: 77 Vol 2		
War Diary	War Diary Of Capt. D Llewelyn Williams R.A.M.C. From-January 1st 1916. To-January 31st 1916. (Volume 2)		
War Diary	St Venant	01/01/1916	23/01/1916
War Diary	Lestrem	24/01/1916	31/01/1916
War Diary	War Diary Of Captain D. Llewelyn. Williams R.A.M.C. From February 1st 1916 To February 29th 1916 77 San Sect. (Volume 3) 38th Div		
War Diary	Lestrem	01/02/1916	17/02/1916
War Diary	Locon	18/02/1916	29/02/1916
War Diary	38th Div 77th Sany Section War Diary Of Capt. D. Llewelyn Williams From 1/3/16 To 31/3/16 (Volume 4)		
War Diary	Locon	01/03/1916	23/03/1916
Heading	War Diary Of Capt. D Llewelyn Williams R.A.M.C. O.C. 77th Sanitary Section 38th (W) Divn From 9th April 1916 To 30th April 1916 Volume 5		
Heading	38th Div 77 San Sec Vol 5		
War Diary	Locon	09/04/1916	19/04/1916
War Diary	La Gorgue	20/04/1916	30/04/1916
Miscellaneous			
Heading	War Diary of Capt D Ll Williams R.A.M.C. O.C. 77 San. Sectn. 38th (W) Divn From 1/5/16 To 31/5/16 Volume 6		
War Diary	La Gorgue	01/05/1916	31/05/1916
Heading	War Diary Of Capt D Llewellyn Williams 77 Sanitary Section From 1.6.16. To 30.6.16. (Volume 7)		
War Diary	La Gorgue	01/06/1916	12/06/1916
War Diary	Robecq	13/06/1916	15/06/1916
War Diary	St Michel	16/06/1916	26/06/1916
War Diary	Le Meillard	27/06/1916	30/06/1916
Heading	War Diary Of Capt. D. Llewelyn Williams 77th Sanitary Section (38 Div) From 1.7.16. To 31.7.16. (Volume 8)		
War Diary	Repumbre	01/07/1916	01/07/1916
War Diary	Lealvillers	02/07/1916	03/07/1916
War Diary	Treux	04/07/1916	05/07/1916
War Diary	Marlancourt	06/07/1916	12/07/1916
War Diary	Pont Remy	13/07/1916	15/07/1916
War Diary	Couin	16/07/1916	28/07/1916

War Diary	Bus	29/07/1916	31/07/1916
Heading	D. Llewelyn Williams Capt RAMC O.C. 77 Sanitary Section 38th (Welsh) Division Aug 1st 1916		
Heading	War Diary Of Captain D. Llewelyn Williams O.C. 77 Sanitary Section 38th (Welsh) Division From 1.8.16 To 31.8.16. (Volume 9)		
War Diary	Esquelbecq	01/08/1916	22/08/1916
War Diary	Peselhoek	23/08/1916	31/08/1916
Heading	War Diary Of Captain D Llewelyn Williams R.A.M.C. O.C. 77th Sanitary Section 38th (Welsh) Division From 1/9/16 To 30/9/16 (Volume 10)		
War Diary	Peselhoek	01/09/1916	30/09/1916
Heading	War Diary Of Captain D. Llewelyn Williams, R.A.M.C., O.C. 77th Sanitary Section, 38th Welsh Division. From 1/10/16 To 31/10/16 (Volume 11)		
War Diary	Peselhoek	01/10/1916	31/10/1916
Heading	D.L. Williams Capt RAMC O.C. 77 Sanitary Section 38th (Welsh) Division.		
Heading	War Diary Of Captain D. Llewelyn Williams, R.A.M.C. O.C. 77th Sanitary Section. 38th (Welsh) Division. From 1st Nov 1916 To 30th Nov 1916 (Volume 12)		
War Diary	Peselhoek	01/11/1916	30/11/1916
Heading	War Diary Of Captain D. Llewelyn Williams, R.A.M.C. O.C. 77th Sanitary Section, 38th (Welsh) Division. From 1st Dec 1916 To 31st Dec 1916 (Volume 13)		
War Diary	Peselhoek	01/12/1916	18/12/1916
War Diary	Esquelbecq	19/12/1916	31/12/1916
Heading	War Diary Of Captain D. Llewelyn Williams, R.A.M.C., O.C. 77th Sanitary Section, 38th Welsh Division. From 1/1/17 To 31/1/17 (Volume 14)		
War Diary	Esquelbecq	01/01/1917	14/01/1917
War Diary	Peselhoek	15/01/1917	31/01/1917
Heading	War Diary Of Captain D. Llewelyn Williams, R.A.M.C., O.C 77th Sanitary Section, 38th (Welsh) Division From 1/2/17 To 28/2/17 (Volume 15)		
War Diary	Peselhoek	01/02/1917	28/02/1917
Heading	War Diary Of Captain D. Llewelyn Williams, R.A.M.C., O.C. 77th Sanitary Section, 38th Welsh Division From 1/3/17 To 31/3/17 (Volume 16)		
War Diary	Peselhoek	01/03/1917	31/03/1917
Heading	War Diary Of Captain D. Llewelyn Williams, R.A.M.C., O.C. 77th Sanitary Section, 38th Welsh Division From 1/4/17 To 30/4/17 (Volume 17)		
War Diary	Peselhoek	01/04/1917	30/04/1917

W095/2550/3
77 Sanitary Section

38TH DIVISION
MEDICAL

77TH SANITARY SECTION
DEC 1915 - ~~DEC 1916~~
1917 APL

To 4 ARMY

San: Sect: No: 77
Vol: I

summarised but not copied
F 1262/1

38 M/Ts

121/7936

S

December 1915
Dec '16

WAR DIARY
or
INTELLIGENCE SUMMARY.
(Erase heading not required.)

Army Form C. 2118.

Place	Date	Hour	Summary of Events and Information	Remarks and references to Appendices
Southampton	4/12/15	2.30	The Section arrived at No 2 Dock Gate and marched to 33 Berth from the tent, in Sections, 1 officer & 27 men & we embarked on the "Hunschow". The 131st Field Ambulance was also on board. It Col. Wills Roberts was O.C. in charge of troops. I brought over the Indt. Officer. The name for the 38th (Welsh) Division	St Williams
		5 p.m.	Sailed from harbour but have - to off the Isle of Wight. The Commanding Officer of the ship was of opinion that it was too rough to cross the Channel.	
		5.30 p.m.	Remained at anchor all day until dusk. Had a boat drill at 12 a.m.	Stur
	5/12/15	4.30 p.m.	Raised anchor & had a good journey across the channel accompanied by a Destroyer.	
Havre	6/12/15	10.a.m	Arrived in Havre Dock and disembarked. Gave up "landing state" to the Prid. Landing Officer and sent a copy to 38th Divisional Headquarters. Deficiency in stores pointed out and obtained from the Ordnance Stores.	Stur
		3.30 p.m.	Section arrived at No 5 Rest Camp.	
		8.30 p.m.	Entrained at No 3 in Company with 131st Field Ambulance, under Major Larry in charge of Staff-Sergeant Evans left behind also the lorries	

Army Form C. 2118

WAR DIARY
or
INTELLIGENCE SUMMARY.
(Erase heading not required.)

Instructions regarding War Diaries and Intelligence Summaries are contained in F.S. Regs., Part II. and the Staff Manual respectively. Title pages will be prepared in manuscript.

Place	Date	Hour	Summary of Events and Information	Remarks and references to Appendices
Aire	7/12/15	10 p.	A.D.C. was. The whole day to travel by road. Detained at Aire and marched 4 or 5 miles to Roquetoire the Divisional Headquarters. The train slowed the O.C. & me the billets prepared for them. The O.C. & is a small farm house to the village & he has rooms at the farm to called May Milor.	S.W.S
Roquetoire	8.9/12/15		Then inspection working at Divisional Headquarters. I visited the San. office of the Guards Division stationed at the Gospe & studied the methods adopted by the San. Section at that station. Received very valuable	S.W.S
	10/12/15		information and hints and reported the results of my visit to the A.D.M.S.	S.W.S
	11/12/15		Visited the Brigade areas and inspected sanitary arrangements & was satisfied that the San. Detachments worked well under very difficult circumstances	S.W.S
	12/12/15		Church Parade 10 a.m. at Beuil - conducted by F.C.	S.W.S
	13/12/15		Visited the Brigade Areas and inspected Sanitary arrangements and Refuse Disposal	S.W.S
	14/12/15		Visited La Gospe & took with me the A.C.O's Hackton for instruction in fitting and carrying arrangements of the Guards Division with a view of starting similar installation for the 38th Division.	S.W.S

WAR DIARY
or
INTELLIGENCE SUMMARY.
(Erase heading not required.)

Army Form C. 2118

Instructions regarding War Diaries and Intelligence Summaries are contained in F. S. Regs., Part II. and the Staff Manual respectively. Title pages will be prepared in manuscript.

Place	Date	Hour	Summary of Events and Information	Remarks and references to Appendices
Roquetoire	15/12/15		Made arrangements for the stationing of 4 sanitary inspectors in 2nd Brigade area, also arranged for the Sg. thing of the men of the 1st R.W.F. and 13 R. Welch Regiment at the Pit-Head Baths near Fosse Blanche.	Itineraries
"	16/12/15		Visited St Venant, where it is proposed to station the 38 (Welsh) Division. It is at present occupied by the 46 Division which is shortly to move to Egypt. There are no Baths & no Laundry arrangements at the present for the troops. Routine work	S.W.
"	17/12/15			S.W.
"	18/12/15		Was present at a gas experiment — men Charges the Shops were made to pass through a trench impregnated with Cl gas. The gas helmets were worn & the results were eminently satisfactory. In the afternoon went with Col A'Mar to St Venant.	S.W.
St Venant	19/12/15		Took the two of the 77 Sandwick to St Venant. Stationed them at the O.C. Bewery on Div. H. Ltrs.	S.W.
"	20/12/15		Superintended removal of Div. H.Q.H.Q & saw to the cleaning of chateaux etc. Took over depôt & offices of the previous San. Lab. that was stationed at St Venant.	S.W.
"	21		Visited the Brigade areas and inspected billets &c; also the Dempfery Sgnd. disinfected a large huts from is which a case of measles to case of Diphtheria had occurred the previous week in another unit.	S.W.S

T2134. Wt. W708—778. 500000. 4/15. Sta J. C. & S.

WAR DIARY
or
INTELLIGENCE SUMMARY.

Army Form C. 2118

Place	Date	Hour	Summary of Events and Information	Remarks and references to Appendices
St Venant	22/12/15		Routine work. Made several unsuccessful efforts to obtain suitable building for a Field hour. Obtained one provisionally by Div. Headquarters.	Steward
"	23		Visited Bethune and Beuglin 21 half-barns suitable for bath thought them to St Venant on my lorry.	Stew.
"	24		Went to Richbad. Newly obtained through our S.A.D.M. six portable baths. These were brought to our bathing establishment. Inspected the 113th Brigade our & the 114 Brigade area and well supplied for the bathing of the Brigade.	Stew.
"	25		Xmas Day. Routine work & Sam. Sect.	Stew.
"	26		Boxing Day. Routine work.	Stew.
"	27		Investigated case of diarrhoea at the 10th & 15th (Welch Regiment) Force 1st to 2nd Bacteriological report, no cause ascertained. Visited O.C. Field Amb. (1,2,3) Brs. and arranged for disinfection of scabies cases &c.	Stew.
"	28		Disinfecting station and Baths (Divisional) completed and bathing and disinfecting established. Visited below & confirmed diagnosis of scabies in the case of a woman of 30 living in an adomevite. Made arrangements for isolation of patient, disinfection of clothes &c — removal of man & children to join home & arranged for Belig. Gen. to place the establishment out of bounds	Stew.

WAR DIARY
or
INTELLIGENCE SUMMARY.
(Erase heading not required.)

Army Form C. 2118

Instructions regarding War Diaries and Intelligence Summaries are contained in F.S. Regs., Part II. and the Staff Manual respectively. Title pages will be prepared in manuscript.

Place	Date	Hour	Summary of Events and Information	Remarks and references to Appendices
St Venant	29/12/15		Visited Brigade Hrs of the 113 Brigade of Infantry in x particular. One case which proved fatal in an Infantist. (Map 36A K 8 d 4.2) The Infantist was placed out of bounds by Brigadier and (about) was disinfected by the Sanit Authority. Other case had occurred a month previous in two adjacent farms. These farms were also placed out of bounds. The Divl. Bacteriologist swabbed the throat of all the actual contacts. In the afternoon I visited with the ADMS the London Artillery Division attached for the time being to the 38th (Welsh) Division & found Sanitation etc. quite satisfactory	Army native [illeg]
"	30/12/15		Visited Robecq & Calonne and inspected Sanitary arrangements of 7 ambulance and troops billeted in that area. Saw portion of an old mill in Calonne which is to be cleaned and converted into a hospital for scabies. Divisional Baths now in field working order. Conference with Col. Ware re Sanitary improvements of billets.	[illeg]
"	31/12/15		Routine work of office. Arranging for taking Sibery Headquarters Orderlies etc. Visited Robecq and inspected a brewery with a view of converting the same to a Brigade Bath House.	[illeg]

Wesely Wigram Capt RAMC
OC 77 Sanitary Section
38th (Welsh) Division

1.1.16

San: Sect: 77
vol 2

38th Div.

Jan 1916

CONFIDENTIAL

War Diary

OF

Capt. D Llewelyn Williams.
R·A·M·C

From — January 1st 1916.

To — January 31st 1916.

(Volume 2.)

WAR DIARY
or
INTELLIGENCE SUMMARY.
(Erase heading not required.)

Army Form C. 2118.

Place	Date	Hour	Summary of Events and Information	Remarks and references to Appendices
St Vaast	1/16		Visited the area of the 114th Brigade and inspected the billets of the 13, 14 and 15th Battalions Welsh Reg. Suggested several improvements.	S/ General Bureau
"	2/16		Inspected sanitary arrangements of the 13th R.W.F. Stationed at Le Sart and decided that latrine buckets not necessary. Short showers trenches answer the purpose.	Ditto
"	3/16		Searched for a place to start baths for Divisional Artillery. Noted a likely space at Haverskerque. Lectured to the officers of the 115th Brigade in the evening.	Ditto
"	4/16		Inspected sanitary arrangements of the 19th Welsh Reg. (Pioneers) and decided that latrine buckets were necessary owing to the soil being water-logged. Cases of mumps occurred in the 15th R.W.F. failed to send to Les Bufs and field-disinfected.	Ditto
"	5/16		Visited the area of the 19th Division & was shown over the Divisional Baths at Lestrem by Col Blythe their sanitary officer. Inspected the Baths at Lestrem field chapelle and Locum.	Ditto
"	6/16		Inspected Rest Station at Merville, also hospitals & Baths at Estrere and Robecq	Ditto

Army Form C. 2118.

WAR DIARY
or
INTELLIGENCE SUMMARY.
(Erase heading not required.)

Instructions regarding War Diaries and Intelligence Summaries are contained in F. S. Regs., Part II. and the Staff Manual respectively. Title pages will be prepared in manuscript.

Place	Date	Hour	Summary of Events and Information	Remarks and references to Appendices
St Venant	7/16		Routine work of section. Accompanied Col Willes to inspect baths at Robecq. Column arrangement working very well. Afs inspecting Brewery at Aire-type received that the place was quite suitable for baths for the Artillery	Alls.
	8/16		Made arrangements with proprietor as to terms of payment for hot water supply. Left a man in charge to prepare the nozzles &c indent for materials from the CRE.	Alls
	9/16		Visited Lestrem and in company with O.C. San Sectn of the 19th Division inspected all the rest[ing] stations and baths sanitation behind the trenches occupied by the 19th Division, also inspected the sanitation of the 1st line trenches	Alls. Alls.
	10/16 11/16		Routine work of section, inspected billets of 113th Brigade Lectured to the officers of the Divisional Artillery and N.C.Os &c of the 115th Brigade Infantry at St Venant & Robecq respectively on Improvements to Billets and the sanitation of baths. Supplies	Alls Alls
	12/16		Routine work. Preparing Billeting facilities for Divisional Artillery Troops	Alls

T2134. Wt. W708—776. 500000. 4/15. Sir J.C. & S.

WAR DIARY or INTELLIGENCE SUMMARY.

(Erase heading not required.)

Army Form C. 2118.

Instructions regarding War Diaries and Intelligence Summaries are contained in F. S. Regs., Part II. and the Staff Manual respectively. Title pages will be prepared in manuscript.

Place	Date	Hour	Summary of Events and Information	Remarks and references to Appendices
St Venant	13/7/16		Inspected the billets of the 17th RWF & suggested improvements needed the Baths at Robecq & Calonne, made arrangements for coal for the latter place.	Illegibly beauly
	14/7/16		Arranged for billeting the 121st Brigade Artillery at Huvezzyne. Inspected the sanitary arrangements of the 120th Brigade Artillery. Fairly satisfactory. In the afternoon visited La Gorgue Laundry with Col. Wills and Major Tugwell.	Illus.
	15/7/16		Bathing of the men of the 120 Brig. Artillery at Haverskerque.	Illus.
	16/7/16		Bathing of the 122 Brig of Artillery at Hyvernizyne & the Machine Gun Company of the 408 Brigade at St Venant. Inspection at Robecq & Calonne.	Illus.
	17/7/16		Lectured to 10th Welsh – Officers & NCOs on Sanitation of Billets at Hemel Brees & 14th Welsh – Regs du linge on the same subject.	Illus.
	18/7/16		Lectured the 15th Welsh on Sanitation of Billets & water supplies & disinfection at Robecq at 3 pm & the 13th Welsh on the same subject at the same place at 5 pm. Discussion followed in each instance.	Illus.

WAR DIARY
or
INTELLIGENCE SUMMARY.

Army Form C. 2118.

Place	Date	Hour	Summary of Events and Information	Remarks and references to Appendices
St Venant	19/6		Visited Isbergues & accompanied Capt Johnson of the 58th Field Ambulance through Hull Chapelle to the Advanced Dressing Stations & then visited & inspected the 6 advanced dressing houses and baths in the forward area. I held hind Regimental Sanita. officers 7. each & 12 men to take over these baths.	S[eesly?] [illeg]
	20/6		16 men of the 129 F. Amb. sent to the forward bns. to make the number up to 5 men in each station.	Ditto
	21/6		Inspected the [?] of the 119th Brig. R.F.A. & found them fairly satisfactory — made several suggestions for their [?] in the afternoon.	Ditto
	22/6		Made an inventory of equipment of baths at Calonrin, Robecq, St Venant and Haverskerque and handed them over to Captain [?] of the 192D[?] [?] who gave a receipt for same.	Ditto
	23/6		Installed men of the San. Sect. at the baths at Longueville Chapelle and Isbergues	Ditto

Army Form C. 2118.

WAR DIARY
or
INTELLIGENCE SUMMARY.
(Erase heading not required.)

Place	Date	Hour	Summary of Events and Information	Remarks and references to Appendices
Lebrun	24/6		Sanitary Section moved from St Venant with Divisional Headquarters. Billeted in the Bocks the O'duty office on the other side of the road.	Steady weather
do	25/6		Made arrangements for the Section. Placed Sanitary inspectors & the three areas occupied by the Division. Took over the tasks at Lobren.	New
do	26/6		Visited the hospitals of the 118 and 115 Brigades. Third Sanitary Section from Vielle Chapelle stationed in Lobren - attached for Sanitary purposes to the 129th Field Ambulance. Col Morgan (ADMS) arranged for a small car to take me about.	New
do	27/6		Visited the Rive baths in the forward area and arranged for improvements and the installation of Lysoes etc. Reports the Bus officer RAB at Jno. & arranged for the bathing of the men	New
do	28/6		3 new W.C.S.T hotpies from 17&18 of Vielle Chapelle regular visits arranged for local Isolates. Shower turned on bus garages with funnels.	New
do	29/6		Ent St Vieil-haire shelled arranged for Lebeny and the prisoners to leave the Faubrey about 300 yards away.	New
do	30/6		Visited all the baths in company with Col Wells Col Morgan.	New

T7134. Wt. W708-776. 500000. 4/15. Sir J. C. & S.

WAR DIARY
or
INTELLIGENCE SUMMARY.

Army Form C. 2118.

Place	Date	Hour	Summary of Events and Information	Remarks and references to Appendices
Lestrem	31/1/6		The Corps Laundry at La Gorgue burnt down. The Baths cannot be supplied with clean clothing. I made temporary arrangements for carrying on a simple laundry for the use of the Division at Vielle Chapelle.	

Signed
D. Llewelyn Williams
Feb 1st 1916.

38th Div.

77. Son Sect.
Vol. 3
38th Div

CONFIDENTIAL

War Diary
of
Captain D. Llewelyn Williams. R.A.M.C.

(Volume 3)

From February 1st 1916   To February 29th 1916.

WAR DIARY or INTELLIGENCE SUMMARY

Army Form C. 2118.

(Erase heading not required.)

Instructions regarding War Diaries and Intelligence Summaries are contained in F.S. Regs., Part II. and the Staff Manual respectively. Title pages will be prepared in manuscript.

Place	Date	Hour	Summary of Events and Information	Remarks and references to Appendices
Lestrem	1/7/16		Artisans & tractor re-helped the tubs at Vielle Chapelle Baths. Found suitable ground at the Brewery for a Laundry and drying ground	H. Lewis Williams
	2/7/16		Plumbers placed 6 stoves & 6 Hypressed iron smoke pipes from Ed and two Sing pipes. Apollo fixed for heating the clothes. The Ironic fixed up a temporary Laundry trestles etc to erect Tub	H. Lewis Williams
	3/7/16		Problem for drying etc. Submitted a scheme for supplying the trestles with pure water & established a list of authorised sources which with an increasing Mess Weary Company of Reordering parole required for stationary the water.	H. Lewis Williams
	4/7/16		Engaged a foreman and 12 women to work at the Laundry of Vielle Chapelle.	H. Lewis Williams
	5/7/16		Visiting the Baths & arranging for Bathing Battalions. Inspected Helps of various units.	H. Lewis Williams
	6/7/16		Sunday. Routine work of Sanitary Section.	H. Lewis Williams
	7/7/16		Laundry at Vielle Chapelle nearly ready - drying ground for order. Inspected & inspected forward farm trestles. Fixed ready.	H. Lewis Williams

WAR DIARY
or
INTELLIGENCE SUMMARY

Army Form C. 2118.

Place	Date	Hour	Summary of Events and Information	Remarks and references to Appendices
Lotheren	8/7/16		Visited the Grenade Division & inspected the Transportable Baths which are now in use in two of this Bdes. Made arrangements for the bathing of the 113th Brigade whose men rest close the 120th Brigade R.W.A.	Illegible William
"	9/7/16		Lecture on Gas attacks & a demonstration on methods of counteracting same were given at Reception Room, Lothren.	Illegible William
"	10/7/16		Inspected the laundry at Vieille Chapelle by 4 tubs. Owing to clean clothing discontinued from the Forgue Laundry for a few days.	Illegible William
"	11/7/16		In view of the move this Division further work, visited the San Sect of the 2nd Division regarding Chang over this place at Bethune.	Illegible William
"	12/7/16		Routine work of Sanitary Section.	Illegible William
"	13/7/16		Routine work of Sanitary Section.	Illegible William
"	14/7/16		Inspecting town of Rolly Laundry & other sanitary arrangements of the Division with the A.D.M.S.	Illegible William
"	15/7/16		Inspecting the rest area & billets of the Division near the front line. New Clothing Store opened at Loun.	Illegible William
"	16/7/16			

WAR DIARY
or
INTELLIGENCE SUMMARY.
(Erase heading not required.)

Army Form C. 2118.

Place	Date	Hour	Summary of Events and Information	Remarks and references to Appendices
Lestrem	17/2/16		Took the D.A.D.M.S of the 61st Division round Lestrem near Vielvorde Chelmsford round the Laundry Arrangements of the Division. He was much impressed by the methods we adopt to overcome difficulties. Everything here to be improvised on the spot.	St Leads Welleny
Locon	18/2/16		Section moved from Lestrem to the new Headquarters at Locon.	St Leads Welleny
"	19/2/16		Routine Work. Pay Parade. Made a tour of the Lys District & found a suitable place for a talk to be erected for the 113th Brigade.	St Leads Welleny
"	20/2/16		Visited Festubert, Vermand, & Robecq.	St Leads Welleny
"	21/2/16		Visited Gorre Laundry — still disorganised. Dismantling the Dying Rooms at Vieille Chapelle & removing the same to Gorre.	St Leads Welleny
"	22/2/16		Artisans of the Section working at the Laundry and Dying Rooms at Gorre and made a start with a new bath. Took a working party to Gorre.	St Leads Welleny

WAR DIARY
or
INTELLIGENCE SUMMARY.
(Erase heading not required.)

Army Form C. 2118.

Place	Date	Hour	Summary of Events and Information	Remarks and references to Appendices
Locon	23/7/16		Revised the Clothing depot. Fine billets Chapelle & deer. Received the inspectors of the Section of the Tourel and Gave respecting. There are considered Locations for the Men to inspect the forward area Fields.	Stanley Williams
	24/7/16		Routine Inspection of Men & Sanitary arrangements also visits to H.Q & Q.M.G new Baths etc	Stanley Williams
	25/7/16		Visit of American Journalists to the Division. Took the Party round the Baths, Laundry & the 130 Field Ambulances	Stanley Williams
	26/7/16		Took Lieut Wynn Jones of the 131st Field Amb to the forward area Baths with a view of taking over the work	Stanley Williams
	27/7/16		from Lieut Raymond Ives of the 129th F Amb.	Stanley Williams
	28/7/16		Routine Work of Section. Inspection of men and Clothing at forward baths. Taking over a Spray bath at Le Quesnoy	Stanley Williams
	29/7/16		Office Work. Closing up accounts etc	Stanley Williams

Stanley Williams
Capt R.A.M.C
A/C 79 a.san HQ

38th Div:

CONFIDENTIAL

77th Sany. Section

War Diary
of.

Capt. D. Llewelyn. Williams.

From. 1 3/16   To 31 3/16

(Volume 4).

March 1916.

77 San.Sec.
38th Div
Vol 4.

WAR DIARY or INTELLIGENCE SUMMARY.

Army Form C. 2118.

(Erase heading not required.)

Instructions regarding War Diaries and Intelligence Summaries are contained in F.S. Regs., Part II. and the Staff Manual respectively. Title pages will be prepared in manuscript.

Place	Date	Hour	Summary of Events and Information	Remarks and references to Appendices
Locon	1/3/16		Routine Work & Inspection	
	2/3/16		Took round the area & the sanitary arrangements of the Division, visited Bray sanitary officer of the 35th Division for instruction.	
	3/3/16		Arranged a Scavenging Scheme for the Township of Locon. A cart to call at all the messes and billets & deliver the refuse to the central incinerator. Billets Surroundings reported clean and tidy.	
	4/3/16		Improved L.Quesnoy Billets & made it suitable for Issuing clean clothes to the men & taking the dirty from them & Sending the same to Laundry.	
	5/3/16		Visited the Corps Laundry & made arrangements to deliver clothing at Locon mon. Le Touret Le Quesnoy Gorre. Interview with the Officer at Merville.	
	6/3/16		Taken on Sgt. Dyne Ints to take charge of Staff of the Baths with men from the 130th Field Ambulance.	
	7/3/16		and arranged for him to take charge of staff	
	8/3/16		Brought 16 tubs at Bethune to place under the Sprays at the Baths. Paid the women working at the Laundry. Visited the Reserve area at Gorse & Hingets and inspected fields with the D.A.D.M.S. Billets good, but some very mucky.	

T2134. Wt. W708—776. 500000. 4/15. Sir J. C. & S.

Army Form C. 2118.

WAR DIARY
or
INTELLIGENCE SUMMARY.
(Erase heading not required.)

Instructions regarding War Diaries and Intelligence Summaries are contained in F. S. Regs., Part II. and the Staff Manual respectively. Title pages will be prepared in manuscript.

Place	Date	Hour	Summary of Events and Information	Remarks and references to Appendices
Locon	9/3/16		Routine work – Gorre & Le Quesnoy visited. Made several reports on area referred to this Section.	See Williams
	10/3/16		Inspected and reported on the water supply by the attached Yeomanry. Removed the V.B. mor from Le Quesnoy Baths.	See Williams
	11/3/16		Routine work of Laundry. Visited Lt Mount & inspected the new Baths and Laundry.	See Williams
	12/3/16		Made an inspection of the Billets in Le Touret area.	See Williams
	13/3/16		Inspected the whole of the new Billets at Rue Spriets & Labouriel.	See Williams
	14/3/16		Made a tour of the trenches occupied by the Division. Found the Vermoral Sprayers and Solution in order but Schofield rollers were arrangements for water supply in the left sector.	See Williams
	15/3/16		A Letto supply. Inspected the water supply at Gonnehem Reserve Area.	See Williams
	16/3/16		Inspected the reserve billets at Guarbéque. Made Forarrein for Le Touret Baths. A new water supply for Le Touret Baths.	See Williams

T2134. Wt. W708—776. 500000. 4/15. Sir J. C. & S.

Army Form C. 2118.

WAR DIARY
or
INTELLIGENCE SUMMARY.
(Erase heading not required.)

Instructions regarding War Diaries and Intelligence Summaries are contained in F.S. Regs., Part II. and the Staff Manual respectively. Title pages will be prepared in manuscript.

Place	Date	Hour	Summary of Events and Information	Remarks and references to Appendices
Loos	17/3/16		Inspection of Billets at La Moulin. Discovered an Artesian well known as the "Grand Fontaine" at La Moulin. But seem shows water to be of good quality.	J Mc C Rev
	18/3/16		Inspected the Billets at Rue du Roi. Found them satisfactory. Provided strongly cutting the new Tunnelling Company with addresses and clarified Inspection of North Paffey at the new Surf. Was unsatisfactory others the presence of Bn a 6th.	J Mc C
	19/3/16		Routine work of Office.	Hardly Rolling
	20/3/16		Inspection of Toilets and surroundings of Reserve Bn. Visiting see air in Billets at Laventie with the R.A. & G.O.C.	J Mc C Rev
	21/3/16		Spent the day inspecting Waterways on the left sector of our line. The present supply was satisfactory. Arranged to tape a fresh supply from an Artesian well 300 or 400 yards away.	J Mc C Rev
	22/3/16		Inspected the Vermorel Sprayer and Water supplies of the Rifle Brig of Kings of Every thing satisfactory	J Mc C
	23/3/16		Took A.D.M.S. of the 61st Division around the Baths, Laundry & the Sanitary Arrangements of the Division	J Mc C

T2134. Wt. W708—776. 500000. 4/15. Sir J. C. & S.

Army Form C. 2118.

WAR DIARY
or
INTELLIGENCE SUMMARY.
(Erase heading not required.)

Place	Date	Hour	Summary of Events and Information	Remarks and references to Appendices
			Away on leave from March 24th to April 7th.	
	23/3/16		H. Llewelyn Williams. Capt. R.A.M.C. O.C. 77th Sanitary Section.	

Army Form C. 2118.

WAR DIARY
or
INTELLIGENCE SUMMARY.
(Erase heading not required.)

Instructions regarding War Diaries and Intelligence Summaries are contained in F. S. Regs., Part II. and the Staff Manual respectively. Title pages will be prepared in manuscript.

Place	Date	Hour	Summary of Events and Information	Remarks and references to Appendices
9/4/1916				

COMMITTEE FOR THE
MEDICAL HISTORY OF THE WAR
Date 9 - JUN. 1916

CONFIDENTIAL

WAR DIARY

OF

CAPT. D LLEWELYN WILLIAMS
R.A.M.C.
O.C. 77TH SANITARY SECTION. 38TH (W) DIVN
FROM 9TH APRIL 1916 TO 30TH APRIL 1916
VOLUME 5.

77 Sander
Vol 5

Army Form C. 2118.

WAR DIARY
or
INTELLIGENCE SUMMARY.
(Erase heading not required.)

Instructions regarding War Diaries and Intelligence Summaries are contained in F. S. Regs., Part II. and the Staff Manual respectively. Title pages will be prepared in manuscript.

Place	Date	Hour	Summary of Events and Information	Remarks and references to Appendices
Locon	9/4/16		APRIL 1916 (Inovenating) Returned late on the night of the 8th from England (Leave). Went round all the baths and the laundry & made a thorough inspection. Found everything satisfactory with the exception that the bathing facilities had not been fully made use of.	Herbelles Wellcome
"	10/4/16		Inspected the village line at Givenchy. The bricks were fairly clean but the sun awnings knotted & story. Refuse, old tins all not buried. Found old tins in sandbags. Gave orders that the whole place was to be thoroughly cleaned.	Herbelles Wellcome
"	11/4/16		Resided at Givenchy. Found the place much improved. Office work.	Herbelles
"	12/4/16		Inspected the village lines at le Touret & Rue de l'Epinette. Found them fairly satisfactory. Found an officer suffering from Chicken pox & had him removed to Lapugnoy Isolation Hospital.	Fosse Wellcome
"	13/4/16		Inspected the water supply of the troops. Found the pipes supply from distillery Rue de Cailloux Brewery very satisfactory.	Les fosses Wellcome
"	14/4/16		Inspected the baths in the reserve with Journal them satisfactory with the exception of a few items which I got attended to Stephan.	Herbelles Wellcome

WAR DIARY
or
INTELLIGENCE SUMMARY.
(Erase heading not required.)

Army Form C. 2118.

Place	Date	Hour	Summary of Events and Information	Remarks and references to Appendices
Locon	15/4/16		Went over to La Gorgue with a view of taking over from the 56th Sanitary Section their premises laundry and baths. Visited Lavantie. Found the baths that refer to be three dismantled part of June.	Heavily Shelling
"	16/4/16		Preparing for the move to La Gorgue	
"	17/4/16		The 77th Sanitary Section moved to La Gorgue. The Lorry had to make two journeys taking equipment stores etc.	Heavily Shelling
	18/4/16		Made an inspection of new area and found that the previous division had left the district in a very unsatisfactory condition. The trenches occupied by this Div. Des Sebens from Picantin to Rue Gurier. Two Brigades in Line Brig. in reserve at La Gorgue. The reserve battalion of the Brigade in occupation are at Lavantie and Fort du Hem.	Heavily Shelling
	19/4/16		Lavantie is a fairly large town very much shelled. Tork daily a train worked. Employed 20 civilian labourers to clean up the town. Latrines of the Sanitary Section put up a bath at the Brasserie, Lavantie	Heavily Shelling

T2134. Wt. W708—776. 500000. 4/15. Sir J.C. & S.

Army Form C. 2118.

WAR DIARY
or
INTELLIGENCE SUMMARY.
(Erase heading not required.)

Instructions regarding War Diaries and Intelligence Summaries are contained in F.S. Regs., Part II. and the Staff Manual respectively. Title pages will be prepared in manuscript.

Place	Date	Hour	Summary of Events and Information	Remarks and references to Appendices
La Gorgue	20/6		Made a thorough inspection of the water supply of the right sector. Found ample & suitable supply. Made arrangements for store of Sterilesten at points accessible to the men for transport to the trenches	Steadily shelling
	21/6		Did the same regarding the Left sector.	Steadily shelling
	22/6		A very wet Sunday. Inspected the district around La Gorgue & more especially the camp of 9th attached Yeomanry. Made arrangements for the purification of water supply at Chevizes Farm.	Steadily shelling
	23/6		Received reports from my Sanitary Inspector from the district. Reported that floors and surrounds were satisfactory but they had difficulty in getting manure removed.	Steadily shelling
	24/6			
	25/6		Investigated several cases of German Measles. Arranged in Fresney for cases to be disinfected.	Steadily shelling
	26/6		Made a thorough inspection of Levente. Eastern places not being satisfactory.	Steadily shelling
	27/6		Improving the water supply of the Town of La Gorgue.	Steadily shelling

WAR DIARY
OR
INTELLIGENCE SUMMARY
(Erase heading not required.)

Army Form C. 2118.

Place	Date	Hour	Summary of Events and Information	Remarks and references to Appendices
La Gorgue	28/4/16		Investigation of cases of infectious disease (mainly) in the troops billeted in the Merville Area & disinfection done after previous cleansing etc. Saw the Road Agent of the Merville Commune and arranged for a water cart to water the streets of La Gorgue.	Already seen
	29/4/16		Inspected the billets, sanitary arrangements etc. of the troops billeted in the Gorgue Area. Made arrangements for the erection of Table, Billans. Visited Latrines in Laventie.	Billans
	30/4/16		Visited St Vennant in the morning. Made arrangements for a drying hut in the event of dragging accommodation in the various Billons. Also by men prohibited from bathing in any but the authorised area.	Already seen

Signed. S. Llewelyn Williams
Capt. R.A.M.C.
O.C. 77th Sanitary Section
38th (Welsh) Division

May 1st 1916.

Army Form C. 2118.

WAR DIARY
or
INTELLIGENCE SUMMARY.
(Erase heading not required.)

Instructions regarding War Diaries and Intelligence Summaries are contained in F. S. Regs., Part II. and the Staff Manual respectively. Title pages will be prepared in manuscript.

Place	Date	Hour	Summary of Events and Information	Remarks and references to Appendices

T2134. Wt. W708—776. 500000. 4/15. Sir J. C. & S.

CONFIDENTIAL

WAR DIARY

OF

Capt D Ll WILLIAMS

R.A.M.C.

O.C. 77 SAN. SECT^N

38TH (W.) DIV^N

From 1 5/16

To 31 5/16

VOLUME 6

WAR DIARY or INTELLIGENCE SUMMARY

Army Form C. 2118.

Place	Date	Hour	Summary of Events and Information	Remarks and references to Appendices
La Gorgue	1/6		Inspected the whole of the trenches occupied by this Division & arranged with the CRE for the water supply to the left in 60 gallon tanks to rail every night. All the water to be taken from authorised sources to be clarified and sterilised. Supplementary supply pumps were also found. Gave instructions to prepare to place 6 Sirdars and a lamp for storage. These supplies are quite near to the men in the trenches.	Stdwash Williams
	2/6		Inspected the water tank of the 129th Res Amb Officers Mess Satisfactory. Inspected also the water tank of the 130th Fd Amb that was not satisfactory. No attempt had been made to chlorinate the water in two of the cabs.	Stdwash Williams
	3/6		Refuse from a glucose factory left in alley heap near 5749, this needs to be a very offensive nuisance. Every permission from owners this has been removed to Fulia and be removed daily to prevent a nuisance. New latrines & urinals constructed at HQ. Was new incinerator to burn the manure.	Stdwash Williams
	4/6		Went round all the tanks with Col Willis. Inspected the	

Army Form C. 2118.

WAR DIARY
or
INTELLIGENCE SUMMARY.
(Erase heading not required.)

Instructions regarding War Diaries and Intelligence Summaries are contained in F.S. Regs., Part II. and the Staff Manual respectively. Title pages will be prepared in manuscript.

Place	Date	Hour	Summary of Events and Information	Remarks and references to Appendices
La Gorgue	5/5/16		Transport wr of the 114th Brigade found it very unsanitary. Gave instructions for burning manure and nothing proper latrines elt.	Stewart Williams
	6/5/16		Inspected the sanitary arrangements of the C Battery 120th R.F.A. Arrangements good. But a large cubbitt facing in front of billet blocked & found creating a nuisance. Gave orders to remedy. In the afternoon inspected the three water carts of the 131 Flam(?). Two showed no traces of U.I. no sterilization. Gave instructions as to proper sterilization of the water. Visited known translation(?). Inspected the trebles-elt in Laventie. Had an interview with the Mayor of La Gorgue regarding the cleaning of the streets. Disinfected premises by Laventie after German removal.	Stewart Williams
	7/5/16		Inspected billets at Merville. Disinfected the transport out of the 113th Brig. at Laventie. Submitted a report on the same.	Stewart Williams
	8/5/16		Inspected the Transport lines of the X/3rd Div'n. found the sanitary arrangements of the turning off the fresh manure well done. Arrangements for the waste supply of La Gorgueisant.	Stewart Williams

T2134. Wt. W708—776. 500000. 4/15. Sir J. C. & S.

WAR DIARY
or
INTELLIGENCE SUMMARY.
(Erase heading not required.)

Army Form C. 2118.

Place	Date	Hour	Summary of Events and Information	Remarks and references to Appendices
La Gorgue	9/5/15		Took over a Cylinder & Water tank from Divisional Cyclists who are leaving the Division to become Corps troops. Paid the civilians, as in number Williams, who are engaged on scavenging work in Laventie.	Lt Hensley Williams
	10/5/15		Inspected the whole of the front line trench sanitation and water supplies. Am accompanied by the S.M.O.R.S.	Lt Hensley Williams
	11/5/15		Inspected the sanitary arrangements of the 113 Brigade at Laventie & installed a tank and cylinder for the water supply of Trench at Chapigny.	Lt Hensley Williams
	12/5/15		Investigated class of Mendes at Mendes, contents segregated and the premises disinfected. Paid of men at 6 p.m.	Lt Hensley Williams
	13/5/15		Inspected the transport lines of the 11th R.W.F. Found them satisfactory and a great improvement on my previous visit when the 15th Welsh were in occupation.	Lt Hensley Williams
	14/5/15		Inspected the water supply of the front line from Winchester to the Rue Pas. Arranged for Clarifiers & Sterilisers at Chapigny Mocquet Trench & am setting tank at Rotten Row.	Lt Hensley Williams

WAR DIARY
or
INTELLIGENCE SUMMARY.
(Erase heading not required.)

Army Form C. 2118.

Place	Date	Hour	Summary of Events and Information	Remarks and references to Appendices
In Gospe	15/5/16		Inspected the billets at La Gorgue. Lectured in the afternoon at the Recreation Room to the Sanitary Squads of the 114th Brigade.	Llewelyn Williams
	16/5/16		Inspected the billets of the battalion 10th & 15th H.L.I. Billets at Duriez. Found them satisfactory. By strong effort by the men is most satisfactory. The use of lime between the Bus of a section is recommended. This tin box stoves to fired to the bed and regarded as billet stoves.	Llewelyn Williams
	17/5/16		Inspected the billets. Own arrangement of 13th and 15th R.F.C. at La Gorgue. Found them satisfactory with one exception. One Bill was slightly then usual. Any of condemned.	Llewelyn Williams
	18/5/16		Accompanied Major Lamont R.E. & arranged to slender rolerry of nightly troops at pumps. Have seen Ihnery firm. The sterilised water to the stored in a two gallon lock & pumped to so gallon tank located in the front line & supplied to french.	Llewelyn Williams
	19/5/16		Met Lt Malimetic of the 12th I. Corps. R.E. & arranged for carrying the concrete trough to conjunction with the pump at Rue Bacquerot with sand bags etc. Also Lt of Canterburg the counter & tank at Rue Hamelet	Llewelyn Williams

WAR DIARY or INTELLIGENCE SUMMARY

Army Form C. 2118.

Place	Date	Hour	Summary of Events and Information	Remarks and references to Appendices
La Gorgue	20/5/16		Took the Plumbers & inspected the Pumps at Muserelt & Roller Row. Found the Champigny Pump working. Got the Pump at Clarges Road started with pumping new panel bags, etc. Arranged to start the work at Pump House.	Stanley Williams
	21/5/16		Inspected the Baths of the 15th Royal Sussex Regt. & 14th R.S.F. Arranged 15th R.S.F. Major Smith offered 15/- for to run water tanks to keep Baths in Proper Running.	Stanley Williams
	22/5/16		Sanitary work in the town of La Gorgue in the morning. Lectured in the afternoon to the Sanitary Squads of the 113th Brigade.	Stanley Williams
	23/5/16		Inspected the sanitary arrangements at Laventie & Fabrick. 13, 14, 15 & 16th R.W. Fus. Payment of the 20 Civilians for scavenging Laventie.	Stanley Williams
	24/5/16		The Kitchens for the Battalions attached at La Gorgue found to be in Good order — most safe & found it tolerable. Provided two Incinerators. Visited Champigny Pump found it working. Pump House unsatisfactory — insufficient water supply — very dangerous. Pump House — the Pump ½ broken.	Stanley Williams
	25/5/16		Found the sufficient arrangement was in progress for a Pumping scheme to Front trench. Champigny cylinder of 400 gallon tank in Powder.	Stanley Williams

Army Form C. 2118.

WAR DIARY
or
INTELLIGENCE SUMMARY.
(Erase heading not required.)

Place	Date	Hour	Summary of Events and Information	Remarks and references to Appendices
La Gorgue	26/5/16		Routine work of Section. Inspection of Sanitary arrangements at Huts etc.	Lt Llewelyn Williams
	27/5/16		Accompanied Capt McKee of the No 3 Bacteriological Lab to the front line. Inspected Lysol at Picantin & cement through sunken road to tent J887. Inspected the water supply Rebri line	Lt Llewelyn Williams
	28/5/16		Saw inoculation. Found the arrangements satisfactory. Inspected water supply at Rue Bacquerot & recommended tent poles to 15th Welsh to look for new supplies in the Rue Tilleloy. Rode to St. Venant. Rode in the afternoon.	Lt Llewelyn Williams
	29/5/16		Took a class of Sanitary men & Company whole of the 115th Brigade. Lectured to their Sanitary duties & arrival of 2 large men in water duties. R.A.M.C. One man from the new from the Machine Gunners into go into food	Lt Llewelyn Williams
	30/5/16		Routine work. Investigated cases of N.Y.D. among civilians	Lt Llewelyn Williams
	31/5/16		Took samples of water from Rue Hyna for Bact Analysis. Inspected the whole of the field belts two battalions at La Gorgue Welling Camp Capt Paul.	Lt Llewelyn Williams June 1.1916. O.C. 77th Sanitary Section

Vol 7 June

CONFIDENTIAL

21 Sanitary Section
RE

War Diary
of
Capt. D. Llewelyn Williams.

From 1.6.16. To 30.6.16.

Volume 7

COMMITTEE FOR THE
MEDICAL HISTORY OF THE WAR
5 AUG. 1915
Date

Army Form C. 2118.

WAR DIARY
or
INTELLIGENCE SUMMARY.
(Erase heading not required.)

Instructions regarding War Diaries and Intelligence Summaries are contained in F.S. Regs., Part II. and the Staff Manual respectively. Title pages will be prepared in manuscript.

Place	Date	Hour	Summary of Events and Information	Remarks and references to Appendices
La Gorgue	1/6/16		Investigated cases of T.F. at Lunestie. Two cases in the Gommes[?] after 61st Div. up for training with the 38th Div. There were 47 contacts d---- the infection who contacted in regiment we tried to Cases in the 38th Div. - the Contacts were removed from the Luraetie Area to the back or reserve area of the 61st Division	Stanley Williams
	2/6/16		Took Col Smith Roberts, acting A.D.M.S. and the regt sector officers front line and examined the water supply at Chapigny Farm Farm Dign Port Luri	Stanley Weeland
	3/6/16		Investigated Cases of Mumps and Munpo at Port du Hem. In the afternoon inspected myself the area of the section with[?] — Inspected Sanderies	Stanley Deans
	4/6/16		Investigated cases of Mumps (4) in the Australian Mining Corps Port du Hem. Cases sent to Hospital — premises disinfected. Contacts under medical observation	Stanley Williams
	5/6/16		Quiet - in ordinary[?] period.	
	6/6/16		Inspected the water supplies, sanitary arrangements of the troops posted at that not[?] Violet Wood Hee Special Walloons forces appropriate to the trenches damaged by Shrapnel - made her[?] & added 2 new into the new scheme of water supply, and the railway line by M---- and Railway	Stanley Williams ----

T2134. Wt. W708—776. 500000. 4/15. Sir J.C. & S.

Army Form C. 2118.

WAR DIARY
or
INTELLIGENCE SUMMARY.
(Erase heading not required.)

Instructions regarding War Diaries and Intelligence Summaries are contained in F. S. Regs., Part II. and the Staff Manual respectively. Title pages will be prepared in manuscript.

Place	Date	Hour	Summary of Events and Information	Remarks and references to Appendices
La Gorgue	7/6/16		Inspection of Troops Posts in the Left. Brig. Sector with special reference to water supplies. Col Mills R.A.M.C. acted accompanied me	Lt Stevenson
	8/6/16		Inspected the field-sanitary arrangements of the 13th R.W.F. I made a special report to the A.D.M.S.	Lt Stevenson
	9/6/16		Inspection of troops Posts in the Right Brig. Sector. No regd. Work.	Lt Stevenson
	10/6/16		Supply etc. Submitted a report. Investigated cases of measles in Laventie. Took around the Sanitary Officer of the 61st Division who is going to take over the Sanitary Work for big Division coming in to this area	Lt Stevenson
	11/6/16		Preparing for a move - probably - clearing up Billets at Huize for being to pay scavenging contracts civilian Labour.	Lt Stevenson
	12/6/16		Sanitary Section moved to Robecq & new Billets with the 130th Field Ambulance	Lt Stevenson
Robecq	13/6/16		Sanitary Section at Robecq.	
	14/6/16		Sanitary Section marched to Raimbert Billets for the night at gas works	Lt Stevenson
	15/6/16		Sanitary Section marched from Raimbert to Saint Michel near St Pol	Lt Stevenson

Army Form C. 2118.

WAR DIARY
or
INTELLIGENCE SUMMARY.
(Erase heading not required.)

Instructions regarding War Diaries and Intelligence Summaries are contained in F. S. Regs., Part II. and the Staff Manual respectively. Title pages will be prepared in manuscript.

Place	Date	Hour	Summary of Events and Information	Remarks and references to Appendices
St Michel	16/6/16		Clearing up new billet and arranging office. Lecture making sanitary arrangements, latrines etc for Headquarters	Hagely Belerang
"	17/6/16		Inspection of fields in New Brigade Area. Improving and supplies et. in New area.	Hagely Belerang
"	18/6/16		Church Parade at H.Q. Arranging Truck at Tingu 1 day of Army of Underclothing for the units of the 114th Infantry Brigade.	Hagely Belerang
"	19/6/16		Arranging Baths for 19th (Welsh) & 10th (Welsh) at Bandlignul	O Rae Belerang
"	20/6/16		Broadening Bivouac of 113th Machine gun company said to be verminous	Hagely Belerang
"	21/6/16		Inspection of sanitary arrangements of the 115th Brigade	Hagely Belerang
"	22/6/16		Sent to the R.A.M.C. report on the water supply of Bruand district.	O Rae Belerang
"	23/6/16		Lectures to section on First aid. Friday a suitable location for a Divisional Collecting Station for the manoeuvres on Sunday 25th	Hagely Belerang
"	24/6/16		Lecture preparing the Collecting Station at Orlencourt Visiting Area of Paris and Eche.	Hagely Williams
"	25/6/16		Sanitary Section opened out the Collecting Station at Orlencourt and acted Hagely as stretcher bearers to the troops engaged. First aid to seeking cases Applying the standard rifle company. The number of wounded wounded & unhandly admitted to the Stations was 164. These casualties came from the Infantry who were not manning the training area.	Hagely Williams

Army Form C. 2118.

WAR DIARY
or
INTELLIGENCE SUMMARY.
(Erase heading not required.)

Place	Date	Hour	Summary of Events and Information	Remarks and references to Appendices
St Michel Le Maillard	26/6/16		Sanitary Section marched down to Le Maillard 20 miles	H Wesley Williams
	27/6/16 28/6/16		San Section stationed at Le Maillard do do	H Wesley Williams
"	29/6/16		Inspection and report on the water supply and sanitary arrangements Le Maillard District	H Wesley Williams
"	30/6		Sanitary Section moving to Rubempré	H Wesley Williams
			H Wesley Williams Capt RAMC OC 77th San Section	
			30.6.16	

July 1916

CONFIDENTIAL

War Diary

of

Capt. D. Llewelyn Williams.
1st. Sanitary Section (36 Div)

From. 1.7.16.   To. 31.7.16.

(Volume 8)

WAR DIARY or INTELLIGENCE SUMMARY
Army Form C. 2118.

(Erase heading not required.)

Instructions regarding War Diaries and Intelligence Summaries are contained in F.S. Regs, Part II. and the Staff Manual respectively. Title pages will be prepared in manuscript.

Place	Date	Hour	Summary of Events and Information	Remarks and references to Appendices
Reboncourt	1/7/16		Investigating source of water supply at Rebencourt – very satisfactory. The whole lot moved to Lafolie marching by night	
Intville	2/7/16		Rating in the morning. Inspection etc in the afternoon	
do	3/7/16		Sunday Inspection etc & the Evening, the Section marched down below to Treux	
Treux	4/7/16		Very wet day – Sunday Section resting	
Treux	5/7/16		Saturday inspection of air tools. Sudden marchals to Morlancourt	
Morlan-court	6/7/16		tested area behind the firing line & found suitable locations for a small collecting station to be worked by the Sanitary Section	
do	7/7/16		Division in action. Sanitary Section opened a collecting station & prepared hut tents first for the wounded. Members of Section acting as stretcher-bearers worked all night until 6 a.m. of the 8th	
do	8/7/16		Rating the Section. 9/7/16 Section standing by waiting for orders. Division again in Action. Sec Section again at the Morning in the Collecting Station gave hot drinks & food to the wounded, members	
do	10/7/16			

T.2184. Wt. W708–776. 500000. 4/15. Sir J.C. & S.

WAR DIARY
or
INTELLIGENCE SUMMARY.
(Erase heading not required.)

Army Form C. 2118.

Place	Date	Hour	Summary of Events and Information	Remarks and references to Appendices
Morlan-court	11/7/16		of the Sectn relief us heaves from the Triangle to Midn Post. Sectn working all night.	Stillards bellowing
do			The same work but at the Try angle, but the Section marched from Midn Post to Morlancourt arriving at the latter place at midnight. along of 9th	Steady hellowing
Morlan-court	12/7/16		Sam. Section left by train for Longpré & from there marched to Pont Remy arriving there 7 a.m.	
Pont Remy	13/7/16		Sam. Section resting	
do	14/7/16		do	
do	15/7/16		Sor. Sectn moved to Conin travelled for a lorry	Stillards bellowing
Conin	16/7/16		Sen. Section working the Bosha, Donzbray Station also at Conin. Attended a Jumping Conference at Marxuen - 8th Corps 4 do. to the meeting was addressed by the L.G. Dir.d. (Lambdin) who	Stillards bellowing
	17/7/16		Reconn Remy. Dine moring with the 1st 4.7 d. Unit arrived to work at the Bosha Buffer Line mon from 130 d. Anul. T. to R Sadly Sectn also 10 mr from 129.7 Anul T. to work at the Clothing Store and Disinfecting Station	Stillards bellowing

Army Form C. 2118.

WAR DIARY
or
INTELLIGENCE SUMMARY.
(Erase heading not required.)

Place	Date	Hour	Summary of Events and Information	Remarks and references to Appendices
Corun	18/7/16		The Book at the Bell taken over by 6 men of the 13th I aunt of the men will be buried at the MDS Clyde Coy. Made arrangements for the inspection of field-etc- by the Sanitary Inspectors.	
	19/7/16		Inspected the whole of the Support lines in the 24th sector & found Sanitary arrangements unsatisfactory & reported accordingly. Making a report on the water arrangements of the District.	
	20/7/16		Inspected the Sanitary and water arrangements of the left sector (support trench) & found them unsatisfactory. There was in a letter Pavelin & Corichin than the right. Thank you. The new front line badly damaged & is now being repaired & reconstructed by our MLB. and Infantry after the bombardment of the recent advance.	
	21/7/16		Inspecting the water supplies of the district.	
	22/7/16		My Orderlies of the San Section making supply of sanitary installations for a Sanitary Exhibition. Fly trap Latrines. Incinerator for burning Excreta etc.	

Army Form C. 2118.

WAR DIARY
or
INTELLIGENCE SUMMARY.
(Erase heading not required.)

Instructions regarding War Diaries and Intelligence Summaries are contained in F. S. Regs., Part II. and the Staff Manual respectively. Title pages will be prepared in manuscript.

Place	Date	Hour	Summary of Events and Information	Remarks and references to Appendices
Krim	23/6		Inspection of Back area. Crispino et. Stones, Krutlhberamy holding villages fairly satisfactory. Acting Opl. 73 Bais sent by order of the Bomb 8th Corps to take charge of sanitary squad at Pieragna Army Headquarters Tandencourt.	
"	24/6		Visited the forward area. Erected the San Stephano in Chambers convenient centres for inspecting the forward area billets & effort lines. Opened another bath at Cervicelli arranged to bath troops in the immediate vicinity. Visited American inspected the laundry which works the clothing not very satisfactory. Found the Kr up to the 152 infantry. Visited the camp & baths at the Zeel, Cavicelly & Trees- at Beaumont & mainly to arrange for the bathing of the	[illegible]
"	25		but Rw.7 at Cervicelli	[illegible]
"	26		Inspected the water supply Afterwards went made an inspection of the new pump at Kings Barn Waterworks in Serenadin found th. to be quite good.	[illegible]

WAR DIARY or INTELLIGENCE SUMMARY

Army Form C. 2118.

Place	Date	Hour	Summary of Events and Information	Remarks and references to Appendices
Étain	27/6		Arranged for the testing of 151 C.B. at Laneville. Inspector Submitted sad report as to quality of the boots of the men and the want of the Division in the Saulain of the area and the head of the Division sent to the front.	Appendix [illegible]
	28/6		Took the Sanitary Officer of the 2nd Division over the area of the 6th Brit. 2nd Division and the Baths. Have had the whole Division and other transported to the Sea before being disinfected by underclothing to the Upper & Baths sent to a Laundry & underclothing & aver of part the No. (2,312 francs) to the Laundry at Amiens.	Major Bell
Bar	29/6		Sgn. Section moved from Bar to Bug. Le Châtre.	[illegible]
	30/6		Water brought from Bar to Bethel before being used. Sgn. Section moved from Bar to Bug. Le Châtre. Water being so bad entailed going to Bethel every morning. The Rhymas Regt. encamped in the Laboral grounds & Lieut Williams of the Lab. Cooped their water supply by the Laboral grounds.	
	1/7/16		Van Echon moved by Motor from Regiment to St. Louis Station. Lorry to Headquarters at Reyneberg.	Heavy steam

Army Form C. 2118.

WAR DIARY
or
INTELLIGENCE SUMMARY.
(Erase heading not required.)

Instructions regarding War Diaries and Intelligence Summaries are contained in F. S. Regs., Part II. and the Staff Manual respectively. Title pages will be prepared in manuscript.

Place	Date	Hour	Summary of Events and Information	Remarks and references to Appendices
			Aug 1st 1916	
			S. Llewelyn Williams
Capt. Raine
OC 73rd Sanitary Sect.
38th (Welsh) Division	

Aug. 1916.   Vol 9

CONFIDENTIAL

War Diary
of
Captain D. Llewelyn Williams.
O.C. 77 Sanitary Section.
38th (Welsh) Division.

From. 1.8.16.   To 31.8.16.

(Volume 9)

WAR DIARY
or
INTELLIGENCE SUMMARY.
(Erase heading not required.)

Army Form C. 2118.

Instructions regarding War Diaries and Intelligence Summaries are contained in F. S. Regs., Part II. and the Staff Manual respectively. Title pages will be prepared in manuscript.

Place	Date	Hour	Summary of Events and Information	Remarks and references to Appendices
Roquetoire	1/5/16		San Section took over the Baths & Laundry at Leggs Cabpel, Wormhoudt & COUTHOVE	S.L. Williams
	2/5/16		San Inspector located at the true Brigade Area. – Bollezeele, WORMHOUDT and COUTHOVE; Inspected the camps at the latter & found many improvements required in sanitary installations.	S.L. Williams
	3/5/16		Col. Barton of the 2nd Army H.Q. DADMS Sanitation visited our H.Q. & gave instructions as to the sanitary requirements – Baths and Army. He left specimens of fly proof box latrines.	S.L. Williams
	4/5/16		Visited WESTHOUTRE and inspected the installation for purifying the discharge from the Laundry, the discharge to be treated (anti Chlorine) in settling tank (Tanko) before released. – apparently quite successful	S.L. Williams
	5/5/16		Started making the same installation at the Laundry WORMHOUDT. Visited the 113th Brigade Area.	S.L. Williams

WAR DIARY
or
INTELLIGENCE SUMMARY.
(Erase heading not required.)

Army Form C. 2118.

Place	Date	Hour	Summary of Events and Information	Remarks and references to Appendices
Esquelbecq	6/8/16		Attended a sanitary conference with the A.D.M.S. at the D.D.M.S. office the Chateau COUTHOVE and made notes of the requirements of the Corps as to sanitary matters. Late in the day inspected the three baths and the two Laundries.	
	7/8/16		Reported on the water supplies of the district. The water in both source & supplies required purifying and conserving. Found a convenient himer near the sinies = YSER. for conversion into a BATH HOUSE for the 115th Brigade. Plans made for the extension of Laundry & additional Drying Rooms at WORMHOUDT	J.L.Williams
	8/8/16		Lectured on practical sanitation to the Officers and NCOs of the 114th Brigade at WORMHOUDT	J.L.Williams
	9/8/16		Inspected the sanitary arrangements of the camps known as K.L.M.N and found several unsatisfactory conditions requiring attention	J.L.Williams
	10/8/16		Lectured on practical sanitation to the Officers and NCOs of the 115th Brigade at (Boesingle) BOESELE	J.L.Williams

WAR DIARY
or
INTELLIGENCE SUMMARY.
(Erase heading not required.)

Army Form C. 2118.

Place	Date	Hour	Summary of Events and Information	Remarks and references to Appendices
Esquelbecq	11/8/16		Took the lorry to MALO near DUNKERQUE. Brought back a load of sand.	
			Lecturing to Officers and men of (1/3) 113th Brigade on "Practical Sanitation" showing special	S.T. Williams
	12/8/16		attention to the requirements of the 2nd army. Gave instructions to the Sanitary Squads of the 13th & 15th B.	S.T. Williams
	13/6/16		& HQ Squad of the 114th Brigade. Rainfine 10 m	
	14/8/16		Inspected temporary Bath at BOLLEZEELE with Col Wills. Inaugurated a school of instruction for the Sanitary Squads of the 115th Brigade. The classes were held in a field	S.T. Williams
	15/8/16		occupied by the 11th D.W.B. Attended a Conference on Sanitation etc. at the HQ 2nd Army S.A. Corps. Got there. Lect at Sanitary School	S.T. Williams
	16/8/16		in the afternoon. Carried out a series of experiments to determine the degrees of hardness produced (wastes) from Laundries, Baths.	S.T. Williams

WAR DIARY
or
INTELLIGENCE SUMMARY.
(Erase heading not required.)

Army Form C. 2118.

Place	Date	Hour	Summary of Events and Information	Remarks and references to Appendices
	18/10		elt after treatment with Chloringluted lime & softening gradually to combine with the fatty acid of the soap so used. The remedying order to that harboured in inspected the sanitary arrangements of the 115th Brigade & found them very satisfactory	J.T. Williams
	19/10		Visited the Sanitary Officer of the 4th Division at Poelhoek with a view of taking over the area	J.T. Williams
	20/10		Took some equipment in the Lorry to PESELHOEK & visited the Camps in this area. Took the Sanitary Officer of the 4th Division	J.T. Williams
	21/10		Sanitary Section moved by train from Eguebecq to PESELHOEK & took over the camps & workshops of the 4th Divisional Sanitary Section. My office on the promenade between Poperinghe and International Corner. A 14.56.4 Sh.1728.	J.T. Williams
	22/10		Inspected the camps in the back area for the battalions at rest. Sanitations made installations for dealing with San Solvente made water from Baths, attention placed etc.	J.T. Williams

WAR DIARY or INTELLIGENCE SUMMARY

Army Form C. 2118.

Place	Date	Hour	Summary of Events and Information	Remarks and references to Appendices
PESELHOEK	23/8/16		Delivered a lecture on "Personal Hygiene and Practical Sanitation" to the 38th Divisional School of Instruction at VOLCKERINGHOVE.	A.T.Williams
"	24/8/16		Inspection of Camps in Forward Area with the D.A.D.M.S., inspected the Canal Bank and front lines of the Left Sector.	A.T.Williams
"	25/8/16		Inspection of Water Supply Sources and submitted a report to A.Q.M.G.	A.T.Williams
"	26/8/16		Sectors working at D.H.Q. — Sanitary inspections, fly trap estimate.	A.T.Williams
"	27/8/16		Visited the Forward Area with the A.D.M.S. & made an inspection of the right Sector front lines and billets of Canal Bank. 9th June Sector.	A.T.Williams
"	28/8/16		Visited & inspected the lines of 16th Welsh & 10th SWB & was accompanied by the D.H.Q. Sent in to D.A.D.M.S. a monthly report on sanitation.	A.T.Williams
"	29/8/16		Inspecting "Billets" Sanitary arrangements on canal bank with Col. Wells (A.H.Q.M.G.)	A.T.Williams
"	30/8/16		Routine Work Experimenting with new fly-killer etc. Very wet and stormy day.	A.T.Williams
"	31/8/16		Inspection of Canal Bank. Took a sample of water from pump.	A.T.Williams

Army Form C. 2118.

WAR DIARY
or
INTELLIGENCE SUMMARY.
(Erase heading not required.)

Place	Date	Hour	Summary of Events and Information	Remarks and references to Appendices
at Irish Farm	31/8/16		Inspected Camps D & E. Supplied several units with fly proof latrine covers. D. Llewelyn Williams Capt R.A.M.C O.C. 77th Sanitary Section	Llewelyn Williams

140/734

Sept 1916

CONFIDENTIAL

WAR DIARY OF

(Captain) J Lewelyn Williams R.A.M.C.

O.C. 77th SANITARY SECTION

38th (WELSH) DIVISION

(VOLUME 10)

FROM 1/9/16 TO 30/9/16

COMMITTEE FOR THE
MEDICAL HISTORY OF THE WAR

Date 30 OCT. 1916

Army Form C. 2118.

WAR DIARY
or
INTELLIGENCE SUMMARY.
(Erase heading not required.)

Place	Date	Hour	Summary of Events and Information	Remarks and references to Appendices
PESELHOEK	1/6		Inspection of sanitary arrangements on canal bank and made arrangements for erecting fly proof latrines to 123 & 124 Co R.E. Visited D camp with Major Shen D.A.D.M.S. the major's horse fell & fractured the septum of his nose. He was taken & dressed at the 31st Amb & over S.w sent off A.T. Serum next morning he was taken from his billet at H.Q. to the 10th C.C.S. at Poperinghe from there he next day train to Bologne	Heavy Showers
	2/6		A report on sanitation of area sent to the A.D.M.S. Inspected the transport lines of the 113, 114 & 115 Brigades & made arrangements to provide the necessary fly proof covered byres for their units.	Heavy Showers
	3/6		Serg B Durris attended a course of instruction in the use of the Box Respirator at the Divisional Gas School.	Heavy Showers
	4/6		Inspected the sanitary arrangements of the 121 Bn R.F.A.	Heavy Showers
	5/6		Inspected Transport lines of the R.E. Companies. Sent in a report to D.A.D as to improvement of washing facilities on canal bank	Heavy rain

WAR DIARY
or
INTELLIGENCE SUMMARY.
(Erase heading not required.)

Army Form C. 2118.

Place	Date	Hour	Summary of Events and Information	Remarks, and references to Appendices
PESHKOPI	6/10		Inspection of camps to the Rear. Are investigating the unlikelihood of any Gunboat Rocks in the forward area of finding that there were no facilities suggested a scheme of forming convenient drying rooms in the transport area of each troops. Also Relios to be made use of in drying the round.	Heavy storms
	7/10		Inspection of camel bank also some of the Transport lines	Heavy storms
	8/10		Attended to the Athletic Brochet dealt with the water works from the Severn by the Destroyhire method at 8 and 2	Heavy storms
	9/10		Investigated a case of "Typhoid" that occurred on the 19th (Wlt) found this the "Schur" wet works at the Dardanelles & the DR Recourt Elevator to the Road lost in control TH-1018, the Reserve crew wounded	Heavy storms
	10/10		Returned to the O.C. See to investigate. Found that the DAC had not turn this morning sent dispatch it near the village reported the matter to the Indian	Heavy rain

Army Form C. 2118.

WAR DIARY
or
INTELLIGENCE SUMMARY.
(Erase heading not required.)

Instructions regarding War Diaries and Intelligence Summaries are contained in F. S. Regs., Part II. and the Staff Manual respectively. Title pages will be prepared in manuscript.

Place	Date	Hour	Summary of Events and Information	Remarks and references to Appendices
POPERINGHE	10/6		Went to Hazebrouck for arrangements for future trip	F.L. Williams
	11/6		Visited the Armoured Train with Col. Willis. Made arrangements for Bath and disinfecting begins for Sirhind Group. Sent to	F.L. Williams
	12/6	9/6	Started a Sanitary School — instruction from 9.30 for the Sanitary squads of the 113th Brigade.	F.L. Williams
	13/6		Inspected the transport lines of the R.F.A. Lectured on Sanitation at Divisional H.Q.	F.L. Williams
	14/6		Visited the 1st 10th & 4th (1nd Divs) Appears satisfactory. Worked Yours & examined the 9.30 for every Jeat is Ock Ames from the old sewerage but at Ypres. The sanitary was not the water the we stated	F.L. Williams
	15/6		Inspected & reported on Artillery lines — Drff.nmine — Satisfactory. Visited Elvenhinghe Chatin with important lines and made Suggestions for the conversion finished to the Divisional Baths	F.L. Williams
	16/6		Investigated the origin of a case of Enteric which had occurred in the 15th R.W.F with negative results. Took the class off work today from the Divisional School my the Sanitary inspection and arrangements at the 130 F. Ambulance	F.L. Williams

WAR DIARY
or
INTELLIGENCE SUMMARY.
(Erase heading not required.)

Army Form C. 2118.

Place	Date	Hour	Summary of Events and Information	Remarks and references to Appendices
PESELHOEK	17	9/16	Church Parade. Capt Goodier, Senior Chaplain officiating. Inspection of P.H. Camps. Reserve Camps all requiring great repair.	St Llewelyn-Williams
	18	9/16	Taking sample of water from the "Cork-Trough" at Queel Baise in isolated huts and submitting it to Hygiene Lab at Hazebrouck for Bact'l Analysis.	St Llewelyn-Williams
	19	9/16	Home on Leave.	
	29	9/16	Returned from Leave via Hazebrouck arriving after midnight.	St Llewelyn-Williams
	30	9/16	Reported to A.D.M.S. and started inspection of area. Weekly sanitary report submitted to A.D.M.S.	St Llewelyn-Williams

1.10.16

St Llewelyn-Williams
Capt. R.A.M.C.
O.C. 77th Sanitary Section.

October 1916
140/875

CONFIDENTIAL.

COMMITTEE FOR THE
MEDICAL HISTORY OF THE WAR
Date -9 DEC. 1916

WAR DIARY of

Captain D. Llewelyn Williams, R.A.M.C.,

O.C. 77TH SANITARY SECTION.

38th WELSH DIVISION.

FROM 1/10/16 TO 31/10/16

(VOLUME II)

Oct. 1916

WAR DIARY
or
INTELLIGENCE SUMMARY.
(Erase heading not required.)

Army Form C. 2118.

Place	Date	Hour	Summary of Events and Information	Remarks and references to Appendices
PESEL#OEK.	1/10/16		Visited the CCS (No3) and was shown cases of "Spirillum Jaundice" also the spirochaete that penetrates the diseases. Kept files also demonstrated the bact. written results of since a fever boy with features of Jaundice suffering from the disease. Several cases have occurred in the Division.	
	2/10/16		Inspected the sanitary arrangements at Canal Bank and arranged to send materials (etc.) up to the field.	Lt Williams
	3/10/16		Very number of (etc.) shelves next safe oft sent to Canal Bank.	Lt Williams
	4/10/16		Inspection of sanitation of Canal bank - great improvement.	Lt Williams
	5/10/16		Inspection of P camp also cafés, troops billets in no area. In the afternoon I made an inspection of Siebels Farm Pionien & found it in fair order. Inspection of sanitary arrangements at Troi Town revealed several defects which required attention	Lt Williams
	6/10/16		Inspected the water supply at Irish Farm and right sector of front line. also took with samples for analyses.	Lt Williams
	7/10/16		Inspection of Reserve Camps and transport lines. Weekly of Lt Baccus report on sanitation sent to the A.D.M.S.	

WAR DIARY or INTELLIGENCE SUMMARY

Army Form C. 2118.

Place	Date	Hour	Summary of Events and Information	Remarks and references to Appendices
Reninghelst	8/10		Analyses fronts at Irish Farm shows gross pollution. A/Cpl J. Brown went home on ten days leave.	J.T. Williams
	9/10		In company with the D.D.M.S. & A.D.M.S. visited the Canal Bank and inspected the huge Dug out where the 177 Tunnelling Company are billetted. Lighted with electricity & fairly well ventilated. Also inspected Divisional the Drying Rooms for the right and left Brigades.	
	10/10		Visited & inspected reserve dumps and transport lines. Was accompanied by the D.A.D.M.S.(Corps) School of Instruction for the Sanitary Squads of the 114th Brigade at D Coy (in the afternoon)	J.T. Williams
	11/10		Visited & inspected Personnel only & was accompanied by D.A.D.M.S. (Corps) School of Instruction for Sanitary Squads 114th Brigade continued.	J.T. Williams
	12/10		Visited & investigated a case of enteric typhoid not occurring in 14th D.L.Bavarian Regt. Nuisance. Platoon S.B. Company 1 Sent sue lives to C.C.S. for further investigation (Bacteriological)	J.T. Williams

WAR DIARY
or
INTELLIGENCE SUMMARY.
(Erase heading not required.)

Army Form C. 2118.

Place	Date	Hour	Summary of Events and Information	Remarks and references to Appendices
PISELHOEK	13/9/16		Visited Irish Farm & reported on the water supply — one of the pumps considered fit for ordinary purposes (water to be boiled).	S. L. Williams
	14/9/16		Inspected the Baggage lines of the R.F.A. Inspection of Waggon lines of R.F.A. continued in the afternoon. Investigated a case of "typhus" in the 17th West.	S. L. Williams
	15/9/16		Examined all the controls at Machine Gun School. Inspected "canteens" and gave instructions concerning 2nd Army Orders which state that all glasses & utensils used for drinking must be sterilised.	S. L. Williams
	16/9/16		Attended a lecture and demonstration at the Gas School. The lecture dealt with administration & the internal economy of units.	S. L. Williams
	17/9/16		Inspected camps in the Back Area, also visited and inspected the village of Proven.	S. L. Williams
	18/9/16		Visited and inspected camel breech belts not of Bridge & also front trenches of right sector. Was accompanied by Lt. Col. S. L. Williams	

WAR DIARY
or
INTELLIGENCE SUMMARY.
(Erase heading not required.)

Army Form C. 2118.

Place	Date	Hour	Summary of Events and Information	Remarks and references to Appendices
PISELHOEK	19	9/16	The D.D.M.S. VIII Corps & the A.D.M.S. inspected D.S.1.D. Dugouts also H. Camp.	J.T. Williams
	20	9/16	Lectures in Sanitation to Billets at the Divisional School. The water truck effected at Canal Bank moved to Longeanne	J.T. Williams
	21	9/16	Accompanied the D.M.S. 2nd Army D.D.M.S. VIII Corps & our A.D.M.S. on a tour of inspection between the water mains camps in the back area & found Expressed himself as satisfied.	J.T. Williams
	22	9/16	Went with the A.D.M.S. to Bailleul & visited the Sanitary Institution at 79 Rue de Lille	J.T. Williams
	23	9/16	Sanitary Section moved from Red camp at A14.d.4.7 to new camp A 14.d.5.0 L the afternoon I investigated suspicious cases of S.F. at Artillery Camp.	J.T. Williams
	24	9/16	The Yperlee Stream on Canal bank flooded & submerged the water trough conveying water. Arranged for the repair of the north bank & the diversion of the stream to the Yser Canal.	J.T. Williams

WAR DIARY
or
INTELLIGENCE SUMMARY.
(Erase heading not required.)

Army Form C. 2118.

Place	Date	Hour	Summary of Events and Information	Remarks and references to Appendices
PESELHOEK	25	9/16	Investigated cases of Typhoid at Canal Bank and Paratyphoid outside at Brielen. (Bolton) R.F.A.)	J.T. Dillury
	26	9/16	Visited and inspected Field and Canal Bank. The recent rains has damaged the dug-outs very considerably.	J.T. Dillury
	27	9/16	Inspected the water supply Canal Bank. Found the trough spouts very dirty. Supervised the cleansing by men of R.A.M.C. men from the ADS. of the D.D.A. Also inspected the chorine of the water of the Ypres at the Canal Locks. Found it fairly satisfactory but suggested a more effective & radical method. Saw tent of the D.A.D.S. through for conveying the water suggests the chlorinator of the taps with S/standpipes faced at convenient intervals.	J.T. Dillury
	28	10/16	Routine work of Station. Deeply Sanitary report submitted	J.T. Dillury
	29	10/16	The San Sct erecting a Stand and Cover for the Inch Disinfector	J.T. Dillury add S.S. J.T. Dillury
	30	10/16	Inspecting Transport Lines 113th Brigade	J.T. Dillury
	31	10/16	Investigating case of Infection Diseases also visited the 1st & K. W. J. at Canal Bank. 1 reported to A.D.M.S. on the 4 cases of Trench feet.	ADS users

Army Form C. 2118.

WAR DIARY
or
INTELLIGENCE SUMMARY.
(Erase heading not required.)

Instructions regarding War Diaries and Intelligence Summaries are contained in F. S. Regs., Part II. and the Staff Manual respectively. Title pages will be prepared in manuscript.

Place	Date	Hour	Summary of Events and Information	Remarks and references to Appendices
			J.T. Williams Capt R.E. O.C. 97th Sanitary Section 3/11 (Welsh) Division	

T.2134. Wt. W708—776. 500000. 4/15. Sir J. C. & S.

CONFIDENTIAL.

WAR DIARY of

Captain D. Llewelyn Williams, R.A.M.C.,

O.C. 77TH SANITARY SECTION.
38th (WELSH) DIVISION.

FROM 1st Nov 1916 TO 30th Nov 1916

(VOLUME 2)

Army Form C. 2118.

WAR DIARY
or
INTELLIGENCE SUMMARY.
(Erase heading not required.)

Instructions regarding War Diaries and Intelligence Summaries are contained in F.S. Regs., Part II. and the Staff Manual respectively. Title pages will be prepared in manuscript.

Place	Date	Hour	Summary of Events and Information	Remarks and references to Appendices
PESELHOEK	1	4/16	Inspected the large Tunnel Dug out on Canal Bank with the D.A.D.M.S. Visited and inspected the Transport Lines of the 113th Brigade	Lt. Williams
	2	4/16	Visited and inspected Camp P - Satisfactory. Also the 115th Brigade Transport lines & found him in good condition. But the 115th Br. Machine Gun Camp & Trench Mortar Battery also their Transport Lines were adversely criticised and reported upon to the A.D.M.S. Recommended the closure of an Estaminet in the Woeston Rd. for non compliance with Army Regulations as to Sterilising drinking cups.	Lt. Williams
	3	4/16	Examined contacts of S.F. at A.D.S. Canal Bank & Inspected proposed "Drying Room" at Machine Gun Farm	
	4	4/16	Out all the morning with the A.D.M.S. Submitted weekly Sanitary Report - Artesian Objections draining the camp	Lt. Williams
	5	4/16	Inspecting the source of the water supply for the Canal Bank at Ypres accompanied by the A.D.M.S. Examined a case of S.F. at 131 F Amb.	Lt. Williams
	6	4/16	Took the Artisans James Buckleys Churchy to Machine Gun Farm & made an estimate of materials for converting a kiln to a drying room	Lt. Williams

WAR DIARY
or
INTELLIGENCE SUMMARY.
(Erase heading not required.)

Army Form C. 2118.

Place	Date	Hour	Summary of Events and Information	Remarks and references to Appendices
PESELHOEK	7	4/16	Examined contacts of Paratyphoid cases in Cardiff City located at Canal Bank — a very exceptionally wet day. Sent Sanity R.A.M.C. orderly to Sanitary Officer — Canal Bank.	J.T. Williams
	8	4/16	Examined contacts of Paratyphoid Cases one at Transport Lines 17th R.W.F. & the other at D. Camp 13th Welsh Regiment	J.T. Williams
	9	4/16	Inspection of the Transport Lines of the 114th Brigade and the units at their Town.	J.T. Williams
	10	4/16	Investigated cases of Dysentery (with the A.D.M.S.) which had occurred in the 12th Rhondda Battalion (Black Watch) Made an inspection of the Canal Bank	J.T. Williams
	11	4/16	Investigated auspicious cases of Dip. in 130 Ant. Located a special Sanitary orderly to each after Tunnel Dug out – Canal Bank – South by newly Sanitary report.	J.T. Williams
	12	4/16	Church Parade. Gave Prophylactic Parade to trachoma inoing Box Resps.	J.T. Williams
	13	4/16	Firing a Clayton Sulphur Disinfector on I Camp.	J.T. Williams
	14	4/16	Conference from Officers & D.A.D.M.S (Sanitation) at O.S. 2610. In the afternoon Invigilated A. case of Paratyph. A at 151 R.B.F.C. at Canal Bank.	J.T. Williams

Army Form C. 2118.

WAR DIARY
or
INTELLIGENCE SUMMARY.
(Erase heading not required.)

Instructions regarding War Diaries and Intelligence Summaries are contained in F. S. Regs., Part II. and the Staff Manual respectively. Title pages will be prepared in manuscript.

Place	Date	Hour	Summary of Events and Information	Remarks and references to Appendices
PESELHOEK	15	4/16	Inspected all the drying rooms of the Division including Machine Gun Coy which has been constructed by the Sen. Section & was accompanied by Col. Page-Turner A.D. & D.H.G.	
	16	4/16	Inspection of Churches & placed 2 men of the Sen. Sec. there for two whole days to disinfect dug-outs.	
	17	4/16	Inspected the Regt. Water Carts.	
	18	4/16	Went on journey to 129 Hamburg Infy (A.M.O.) Visited the Govn. Army Sanitation and Personal Hygiene at Divisional School	
	19	4/16	Church Parade. Disinfection of the house of the two German	
	20	4/16	The R.J.A. dugger line. Inspection of camps with Depty. Adjutant. Investigating case of Diphtheria at 130 J. Aust — it turned out to be negative.	
	21	4/16	Inspection of R.J.A. Camps with Capt Ambler D.A.D. and (Army) Visited the Sen. Water Carp and inspected Bayley's Apparatus.	
	22	4/16	Surgeon General Porter, D.M.S. 2nd Army visited the workshops and inspected the camp of the Sanitary Section. I made an inspection of the camps at Bleuerdinghe Chateau & Mackeron Farm.	

Army Form C. 2118.

WAR DIARY
or
INTELLIGENCE SUMMARY.
(Erase heading not required.)

Instructions regarding War Diaries and Intelligence Summaries are contained in F. S. Regs., Part II. and the Staff Manual respectively. Title pages will be prepared in manuscript.

Place	Date	Hour	Summary of Events and Information	Remarks and references to Appendices
PESELHOEK	23	4/16	I inspected the sanitation of the trenches front line & support trenches of the right brigade front. Found them satisfactory	J.T. Williams
	24	4/16	D.A.D.M.S. (sanitary) accompanied me to Canal Bank & we made an inspection of the billets (dug-outs), sanitary arrangements, also the water supply to the large tunnel dug-outs. Attention was drawn to the defective ventilation of 2 of these dug-outs. The remainder (76) were well ventilated. Both air shafts from the dug-out to the surface. The work of ventilating the 16 is proceeding.	J.T. Williams
	25	4/16	Inspection of 151 & R.E. Throughout revealed the fact that there were several unsatisfactory latrines. These are to be remedied. Weekly report submitted.	J.T. Williams
	26	4/16	Church Parade. Camps [illegible]	
	27	4/16	Inspected the Billets (an arrangement of the Oh Debel at Ypres. Removed my party from a wet cellar	J.T. Williams
	28	4/16	Inspected the French front line which is to be taken over by 39th Divn. There were no sanitary arrangements.	J.T. Williams

WAR DIARY
or
INTELLIGENCE SUMMARY.
(Erase heading not required.)

Army Form C. 2118.

Place	Date	Hour	Summary of Events and Information	Remarks and references to Appendices
PESELHOEK	29	11/16	Investigated the water supply of the area evacuated by the 13th enck troops & report occupied by a brigade of the 39th Division. Special report sent to A.D.M.S. †	S.I. Seeram
	30	4/16	Inspected the following camps C.D.C.T. also E camp which is now occupied by the 17th R.F.A. This is a Corps camp & does not come up to the standard of the 38th Division. I suggested the necessary improvements. Sent a Water Corporal to A Battery 121 R.F.A. & trained water men to C Battery 121 R.F.A.	S.I. Seeram

† To replace unavailable men.

D. Llewelyn Williams Capt. R.A.M.C.
O.C. 77th Sanitary Section.

CONFIDENTIAL.

Vol 13

'40/903

WAR DIARY of

Captain D. Llewelyn Williams, R.A.M.C.,

O.C. 77TH SANITARY SECTION.

38th (WELSH) DIVISION.

(VOLUME 13)

FROM 1st Dec. 1916 TO 31st ~~25th~~ Dec. 1916

COMMITTEE FOR THE
MEDICAL HISTORY OF THE WAR

Date 31 JAN. 1917

Army Form C. 2118.

WAR DIARY
or
INTELLIGENCE SUMMARY.
(Erase heading not required.)

Instructions regarding War Diaries and Intelligence Summaries are contained in F. S. Regs., Part II. and the Staff Manual respectively. Title pages will be prepared in manuscript.

Place	Date	Hour	Summary of Events and Information	Remarks and references to Appendices
ROSELHOEK	1	1/6	Major Genl Chichester 2nd Army, Brig Genl Atkinson GS & R Corps accompanied by a French General & his staff visited 20 F.L. Camps & were shown the Baths and all the Sanitary incl dating. Expressed their satisfaction with what they saw.	
"	2	1/6	Submitted weekly sanitary & water reports to ADMS. Routine	J L Williams
"	3	1/6	Inspection of Baths at Wieltje Halion & also fields where new men taken over by the 118th Brigade of the 39 RD were supplied them with 50 Latrine boxes	J L Williams
"	4	1/6	Visited Gravel Dump and changed the Inspector.	J L Williams
"	5	1/6	Routine work of Section.	J L Williams
"	6	1/6	Lectured morning and afternoon at the Army School of Sanitation Hagebrouck on Practical Sanitation.	J L Williams
"	7	1/6	Visited Reserve Area with the ADMS and reported in Laundry and Bathing Accommodation to A.A. Q.M.G.	J L Williams
"	8	1/6	Sanitary Section of the Corps inspected by G.O.C. of 2C Divn who expressed himself as satisfied with the work of Sanitary of the section.	J L Williams

WAR DIARY
or
INTELLIGENCE SUMMARY.
(Erase heading not required.)

Army Form C. 2118.

Place	Date	Hour	Summary of Events and Information	Remarks and references to Appendices
RESELHOEK	9	12/16	Visited and inspected the trenches and back billets of the 116 Brigade. Left sector taken over by the French & now occupied by the 39th Division. Sent in weekly sanitary report.	
	10	12/16	Supplied the above sector with meat safes, chloride of lime.	
	11	12/16	Took the Sanitary Officer of the 39 R Division over the back and front area.	
	12	12/16	Routine work of Section.	
	13	12/16	Took S.R.M.S of the 8th Corps over the Disinfecting Stations which were open.	
	14	12/16	Went to Hazebrouck in the morning, brought back my Sanitary Inspector to be inspected by the Corps Commander. Section moved from Roselhock to Boquelberg.	
	15	12/16	I spent the day at Hazebrouck lecturing on Practical Sanitation at the Army School of Sanitation.	
	16	12/16	Inspected the area occupied by the 114 Brigade. Water also the artillery area at Houtkerque, Herzeele, also the 113th Brigade at Boland.	
	17	12/16	Sent the Jones to disinfect blankets at Boland. Visited Poree (Cpl Schier)	

Army Form C. 2118.

WAR DIARY
or
INTELLIGENCE SUMMARY.
(Erase heading not required.)

Instructions regarding War Diaries and Intelligence Summaries are contained in F. S. Regs., Part II. and the Staff Manual respectively. Title pages will be prepared in manuscript.

Place	Date	Hour	Summary of Events and Information	Remarks and references to Appendices
PEEHOER ESQUELBECQ	18th	12/16	Visited and inspected the camps of the 113th Brigade at Boesele. I was accompanied by the acting A.D.M.S. of the Division (Colonel Roberts)	Lt. Williams
	19th	12/16	Visited the camps - support lines etc of the 115th Brigade in the left sector. Billets and sanitation greatly improved. Capt Ivon Ivans R.A.M.C. in charge of the Brigade.	Lt. Williams
	20th	12/16	Lectured at the Army School of Sanitation, Hazebrouck on Practical Sanitation morning and afternoon.	Lt. Williams
	21st	12/16	Inspection of sanitary arrangements at Eequelberg. Lectured at the Corps School and visited to return of commanding officers.	Lt. Williams
	22nd	12/16	Office work in the morning. Inspection of Billets and of Boesele Camp. Hd 115th Infantry Brigade	Lt. Williams
	23rd	12/16	Inspection (Sanitary) arrangements of the Brigade of Artillery - very careful. Sorry to send to part of material. Found note for a hook at Hazauh	Lt. Williams
	24th	12/16	Visit from A.D.M.S. (Sanitation) regarding the issue of Lorflet and sanitary installation at Lucas Day	Lt. Williams
	25th		Home on Leave till Jan 9th	Llewellyn Williams Capt R.A.M.C. O.C 77 F San Sec

26/12/16

Army Form C. 2118.

WAR DIARY
or
~~INTELLIGENCE SUMMARY.~~
(Erase heading not required.)

Instructions regarding War Diaries and Intelligence Summaries are contained in F. S. Regs., Part II. and the Staff Manual respectively. Title pages will be prepared in manuscript.

Place	Date	Hour	Summary of Events and Information	Remarks and references to Appendices
ESQUELBECQ	26/12/16		Capt Williams O.C. the unit went on leave. Capt Theobon R.A.M.C. assumed duties of Acting O.C. went to BOLLEZEELE to inspect a new water supply at A.23.d.7.6 (Sh 27). Samples to be analyzed. Should prove a valuable source next summer.	J.W.S.
do.	27/12/16		Morning visited 122 Bde R.F.A. All trenches latrine not provided with flyproof covers. A large urine, a billet of B Battery, was found to be badly ventilated. Attention was drawn to this need for opening the windows regularly. Afternoon visited HERZEELE to judge as to best site for a Bathhouse. Here for Artillery. Original site chosen at D.10.c.2.3 considered best.	J.W.S.
do.	28/12/16		Morning inspected baths etc at HERZEELE and saw work commenced. Then inspected the lines and billets of the 35th D.A.C. - Conditions remarkably good in circumstances. Afternoon to BERQUES to see Officer of No 10 Sect N Field Engineers. The French Army as use of the well at BOLLEZEELE by our troops.	J.W.S.
do.	29/12/16		Morning inspected billets of 13 R.W.F. and 15 R.W.F. at BOLLEZEELE. Took of material a bar to insanitary conditions. Samples	J.W.S.

WAR DIARY or INTELLIGENCE SUMMARY

Army Form C. 2118.

Place	Date	Hour	Summary of Events and Information	Remarks and references to Appendices
ESQUELBECQ	29/12		for chemical and bacteriological analysis taken from well at A23d 7.6. Afternoon French Officer left word this well could be used when supply allowed use by Troops and the French Railway Engine.	
do.	30/12		Morning inspected with Adjutant, R.E., a site for a bathhouse in ESQUELBECQ for D.H.Q. Troops. Claims Officer also present and took details re hiring. Inspected work on baths at HERZEELE. Afternoon, work commenced on ESQUELBECQ bathhouse. Six Spray boilers brought from drying room POPERINGHE. Samples from BOLLEZEELE well sent to No1 Mobile Lab 10 C.C.S. for bacteriological analysis. Work at HERZEELE Baths progressing favourably. Chemical analysis of Bollezeele water made in this unit — very good water.	

Army Form C. 2118.

WAR DIARY
or
~~INTELLIGENCE~~ SUMMARY
(Erase heading not required.)

Instructions regarding War Diaries and Intelligence Summaries are contained in F. S. Regs., Part II. and the Staff Manual respectively. Title pages will be prepared in manuscript.

Place	Date	Hour	Summary of Events and Information	Remarks and references to Appendices
ESQUELBECQ	31/12		Morning, visited huts in ESQUELBECQ and found work progressing favourably, also HERZEELE huts and found these nearing completion. Prepared the way for an agreement with owner of barn re. hire of the premises as a bath. Afternoon agreement signed with owner of bath in ESQUELBECQ as to hire at 1 franc per day. Translation sent to Claims Officer for filing, copy with me & copy with owner.	J.R.M [signed] Captain act/O.C. 77 San Sectn

CONFIDENTIAL.

WAR DIARY of

Captain D. Llewelyn Williams, R.A.M.C.,

O.C. 77TH SANITARY SECTION.

38th WELSH DIVISION.

(VOLUME 14)

FROM 15 TO 31st

COMMITTEE FOR THE
MEDICAL HISTORY OF THE WAR
Date 13 MAR. 1917

WAR DIARY
or
INTELLIGENCE SUMMARY.
(Erase heading not required.)

Army Form C. 2118.

Place	Date	Hour	Summary of Events and Information	Remarks and references to Appendices
ESQUELBECQ	1/7		Saw work at ESQUELBECQ Baths with Lt Batho. Attended A.D.M.S. office rest of day.	A.M.W.
do	2/7		A.D.M.S. being away inspecting Mustering camp at HOULLE. Inspected BOLLEZEELE area in response to request. P/15 Bole. Such of Material chit room for backward sanitary condition. In afternoon, in company with Adjutant C.R.E. inspected to-huts-in ESQUELBECQ and HERZEELE under construction. Agreement for hiring premises at HERZEELE arranged at 1 Franc per day by Billeting Offer - Copy Payne 16 Claim.	A.M.W.
do	3/7		Inspected 1 & 2 Camps in morning in accordance with letter of Corps Commander. Objective greenchops the remedies. Also saw hutted 1/3F T.M.Bs. at HOUDKERQUE - found them in very good sanitary condition. Office work - Sanitary section.	A.M.W.
do	4/7		Captain Williams in orders having been wounded.	
do	5/7		Gas. Attended a medical Board "A.D.M.S." on an officer at-with MERKEGHEM and on T.O. Men at BOLLEZEELE. In afternoon inspected with A.D.M.S. Divisional School at J Camp - found all in order; as far as cold be expected.	A.M.W.

Army Form C. 2118.

WAR DIARY
or
INTELLIGENCE SUMMARY.
(Erase heading not required.)

Place	Date	Hour	Summary of Events and Information	Remarks and references to Appendices
ESQUELBECQ	6/7		Visited MOULLE to investigate case of Measles reported by R.W.F. an officer. S.M.O. & other had case in hand & all precautions taken.	
	7/7		Visited POPERINGHE to see Capt. Berkeley Cole R.A.M.C. Commandant of 9th Corps School of Sanitation. Anxious of syllabus for school. Opened with Captain & shown returns. Afternoon Office work.	
	8/7		Visited HOUDKERQUE in morning to attend a F.G.C.M. on B.Q.M.S. Fenner & far Sergt Shaw of the 19 A.C. Court adjourned. Office work in afternoon. Note from no 1 Mobile Lab - no answer, can he examine there - only at HAZEBROUCK. Capt.	
	9/7		Visited HERZEELE with DADMS. inspected Baths. Office work. Afternoon - Capt. J.L. Williams M.C. R.A.M.C. returned - evening	

Signed G.R.Shrosh.
Capt. R.A.M.C.
acting DDMS 77 Sanitarian
26/6 to 8/7

Army Form C. 2118.

WAR DIARY
or
INTELLIGENCE SUMMARY.
(Erase heading not required.)

Instructions regarding War Diaries and Intelligence Summaries are contained in F. S. Regs., Part II. and the Staff Manual respectively. Title pages will be prepared in manuscript.

Place	Date	Hour	Summary of Events and Information	Remarks and references to Appendices
Eguelbecq	9	7/17	Returned from leave and was luckily broken up by the storm. Car at Calais. Reached Eguelbecq at 8 p.m.	J.L. Williams
	10	7/17	Visited the Corps School at Aulthuwe also had a conference with the Sanitary Officer of Poperinghe re starting Sanitary Lectures for N.C.O.s and men.	J.L. Williams
	11	7/17	Lectured on Field Sanitation at the Army School, Hazebrouck.	J.L. Williams
	12	7/17	Inspection of the Sanitary arrangements & Sick units of the 115th Brigade stationed at Borrecul and found them much improved also examined the water supply of a deep well which seems out to be of good quality and ample in quantity.	J.L. Williams
	13	7/17	Visited Hazebrouck & went through some Sanitary papers with D.A.D.M.S. (Sanitation) 2nd Army	J.L. Williams
	14	7/17	Sanitary Section broking up; a lot of equipment sent to Wardreck. I attended a conference of Corps School Sanitation at Poperinghe	J.L. Williams
Poelhoek	15	7/17	Sanitary Section moved from Eguelbecq to camp at Poelhoek & in the afternoon I visited Cannel Bank & found the water supply disorganised owing to the flooding of the troughs. Units very well ca____	J.L. Williams

T2134. Wt. W708—776. 500000. 4/15. Sir J.C. & S.

Army Form C. 2118.

WAR DIARY
or
INTELLIGENCE SUMMARY.
(Erase heading not required.)

Instructions regarding War Diaries and Intelligence Summaries are contained in F.S. Regs., Part II. and the Staff Manual respectively. Title pages will be prepared in manuscript.

Place	Date	Hour	Summary of Events and Information	Remarks and references to Appendices
PESELHOEK	16	17	Lectured on "Water Supply" at the Corps School of Sanitation. Poperinghe. Lacy Bn. Doris gave a demonstration on the Water Cart. 2 Inspectors located at Canal Bank and 2 at Lovey Farm. These men will supervise the sanitation of the Brigades in the front area.	Lt Williams
	17	17	Lectured on "Practical Sanitation" at the Army School of Sanol. Huge bank. Serg Bacok R.A.M.C. returned with me and is now attached to the Section. Experiment on the value of dry heat at 60°C to destroy vermin	Lt Williams
	18	17	Visited Canal Bank with Col Morgan. Investigated the contacts of 2 cases of Typhoid in 1/3 & 2 and 6/13 RWF respectively. Sent one who had Typhoid some years previously to a CCS for Fact Examination.	
	19	17	Serg White made a plan of the proposed "Bath House" to be constructed for troops in the forward area. Situated in Canal Bank. I made a report on the Disinfecting Dumps R.I.C. & Disinfector at Canal Bank and made a report on the Disinfecting appliances sent to Canal Bank. A lorry load of sanitary appliances sent to Canal Bank	Lt Williams
	20	17	Working Parts from Section repairing and altering the old French Sth 113th Brigade Canal Bank. Repaired Several Camps in Peckman	Lt Williams

Army Form C. 2118.

WAR DIARY
or
INTELLIGENCE SUMMARY.
(Erase heading not required.)

Instructions regarding War Diaries and Intelligence Summaries are contained in F. S. Regs., Part II. and the Staff Manual respectively. Title pages will be prepared in manuscript.

Place	Date	Hour	Summary of Events and Information	Remarks and references to Appendices
PESELHOEK	21	7/17	Working Party at Canal Bank. Section Cleaning up of the Camp. Church Parade. Inspected the Waggon lines of Bu 121 & 122 Br R.F.A.	Lt T. Williams
	22	7/17	Spent the day inspecting all the camps with the Camp Adjutant and making notes of necessary improvements and sanitary appliances, the latter supplied from the Sanitary Section workshop.	Lt T. Williams
	23	7/17	Lectured on Water Supply at the Corps School. Papers up in the morning and visited the forward left sector in the afternoon.	Lt T. Williams
	24	7/17	Lecturing morning and afternoon at Hazebrouck. Practical available. Section inspecting & conducting sanitary appliances as usual.	Lt T. Williams
	25	7/17	Conducting experiment at the Lazarini in to the efficacy of Steam at 50°C for destroying lice and ova. Sergeant Vescock form transvering.	Lt S. Thomas
			In the afternoon inspected Canal bank with Lt Banks R.E.	Lt Banks R.E.
	26	7/17	Inspection of Camps in proene area. Lectured on Sanitation (Overseer Shops) at Corps	Lt S. Thomas
	27	7/17	Plumbers of Section including Sub R. L. at A.14. OC inspecting D.E. Corps. Sent in weekly Sanitary report to A.D.M.S.	
	28		Sanitary Conference at Hazebrouck where new scheme of sanitation was explained & discussed by OC Sain Sections of 2nd Army.	F. L. Aldring

T2134. Wt. W708—776. 500000. 4/15. Sir J. C. & S.

Army Form C. 2118.

WAR DIARY
or
INTELLIGENCE SUMMARY.
(Erase heading not required.)

Instructions regarding War Diaries and Intelligence Summaries are contained in F. S. Regs., Part II. and the Staff Manual respectively. Title pages will be prepared in manuscript.

Place	Date	Hour	Summary of Events and Information	Remarks and references to Appendices
PESELHOEK	29	—	Inspection of Inf. Camps in the morning. Latrines insanitary and inadequate. New latrines recommended by the Section. Visited and inspected the left Section in the afternoon with the A.D.M.S.	J. Williams
	30	—	Lectured on D.E. Supply at VIII Corps School in the morning. Demonstration in the Water Cart (Lewis) in the afternoon.	J. Williams
	31	—	OC lectured on Practical Sanitation at Army School Hazebrouck, also attended conference in the afternoon of re. to the duties of Sanitary Police Group on work the unit construction work and inspecting duties.	J. Williams

Signed J Llewelyn-Williams
Capt. RAMC
OC 17th Sanitary Section.

CONFIDENTIAL.

WAR DIARY of

Captain D. Llewelyn Williams, R.A.M.C.,

O.C. 77TH SANITARY SECTION.

38th (WELSH) DIVISION.

(VOLUME 15)

FROM 1/2/17 TO 28/2/17

140/1991 Vol 15

COMMITTEE FOR THE
MEDICAL HISTORY OF THE WAR
Date 4 — APR. 1917

Army Form C. 2118.

WAR DIARY of 77th San: Secn.

INTELLIGENCE SUMMARY. (Volume 15)

1st to 28th Feb 1917

(Erase heading not required.)

Instructions regarding War Diaries and Intelligence Summaries are contained in F.S. Regs., Part II. and the Staff Manual respectively. Title pages will be prepared in manuscript.

Place		Date	Hour	Summary of Events and Information	Remarks and references to Appendices
PESELHOEK	1	2/17		In the morning conducted experiments with steam in a chamber at a temp of 55°C to see its effect on lice & their ova. The experiments were carried out by Sergeant Pocock from the 2nd Army H.Q. & was attached to the 77th Sanitary Section. Successful	Lt Williams
	2	2/17		Inspection of H.Q. camps. Found the latter insanitary & overcrowded. Suggested several improvements. Every Cond & sanitary appliances made at workshops sent to Kept Sectn. and Canal Bank.	Lt Williams
	3	2/17		Drew money from Field Cashier. Paid the men. Inspected the L. Defences and Machine Gun Farm.	Lt Williams
	4	2/17		Investigated the contacts of a case of Typhoid, in the 15th Welsh, no suggestion of a "carrier" found. I visited 2 or 3 miles north-east the last evening. Col Morgan as A.D.M.S. of the 38th Division. Introduced to the new A.D.M.S.	Lt Williams
	5	2/17		Inspecting all the billets along the Elverdinghe Rd. Found several unsatisfactory features and suggested improvements.	Lt Williams
	6	2/17		Lecturing at the School, Poperinghe. (Wells supply) Inspection of chief nearby supplies also frogs but the Poperinghe the Essendinck supplies.	Lt Williams
	7	2/17		Lecturing on Practical Sanitation at the 2nd Army School, Poperinghe.	Lt Williams

WAR DIARY
or
INTELLIGENCE SUMMARY.
(Erase heading not required.)

Army Form C. 2118.

Instructions regarding War Diaries and Intelligence Summaries are contained in F.S. Regs., Part II. and the Staff Manual respectively. Title pages will be prepared in manuscript.

Place	Date	Hour	Summary of Events and Information	Remarks and references to Appendices
PESELHOEK	8	2/7	Routine work of Sanitary Section. Visited & inspected units in Brigade District	Lt Williams
	9	2/7	The Section visited and addressed by the new A.D.M.S. (Col. Gill) & also inspected camp & workshops etc. In the afternoon I inspected the Lift Sects. of our front line with the A.D.M.S.	Lt Williams
	10	2/7	Visited baths, drying rooms & inspected all sanitary arrangements on Canal bank with the A.D.M.S. Section constructed a new fly-proof latrine at G camp.	Lt Williams
	11	2/7	Investigated news of much of 130 Field Ambulance. Also reported on a "well" at Three Rings Farm. Lieut. Jones off return night of right Lunge.	Lt Williams
	12	2/7	Visited & inspected L. & E. camps & sent in report to A.D.M.S. suggested a complete change in the system of latrines. Lectured in the afternoon Corps School	Lt Williams
	13	2/7	Lectured on water supply at Corps School. Demonstrated bals. East at 6am at J. Farm & at Terry Farm to Regimental Medical Officers.	Lt Williams
	14	2/7	Lectured at Army School of Sanitation, Hazebrouck	Lt Williams
	15	2/7	Inspection of Left Brigade (Forward area & reserve)	Lt Williams
	16	2/7	Invest of Pontypool in 16 Welsh R/Depending in 19 Welsh R (Relieve from	Lt Williams

Army Form C. 2118.

WAR DIARY
or
INTELLIGENCE SUMMARY.
(Erase heading not required.)

Instructions regarding War Diaries and Intelligence Summaries are contained in F. S. Regs., Part II. and the Staff Manual respectively. Title pages will be prepared in manuscript.

Place	Date	Hour	Summary of Events and Information	Remarks and references to Appendices
PEZELHOEK	17	2/17	Attended a conference of Staff Captains & Quartermasters. Col Ryerson	S.L.Williams
	18	2/17	Meeting - dealing with administration & internal economy of units. Church Parade. Routine Work of Section.	S.L.Williams
	19	2/17	Visits c/out divn. Past the men. Lectures on Sanitation at the Corps School	S.L.Williams
	20	2/17	In the morning lectured on Water Supplies at the Corps School. Investigated & examined metallic contacts at 130 F. Ambulance. In the afternoon investigated the water supply at Cruels Bank and submitted a report to the A.D.M.S	S.L.Williams
	21	2/17	Staff Sergeant White showed plans for an officers' Bath at Siverdinghe. Lectured at Army School, Hazebrouck on Practical Sanitation	S.L.Williams
	22	2/17	Investigating Typhoid Contacts. M/Sgts 164 (Welch) & Sent on men H.C.C. for Inoculation. Reminder Troops with the M.Os. of the 10th & 11th S.W.B. of Borough Village	S.L.Williams
	23	2/17	Spent the morning with A.A.G in Inspecting Baths & Laundries.	S.L.Williams
	24	2/17	Lectured at Hazebrouck in the morning & investigated cases of measles in the afternoon.	S.L.Williams
	25	2/17	Church Parade. Usual Routine. Demonstration on water cart Disinfection	S.L.Williams

Army Form C. 2118.

WAR DIARY
or
INTELLIGENCE SUMMARY.
(Erase heading not required.)

Place	Date	Hour	Summary of Events and Information	Remarks and references to Appendices
PESELHOEK	26	2/7	Visited and inspected the camp of the 151 R.E. and found it greatly improved. Inspected D and E camps and suggested several improvements which will shortly be carried out.	J.T.Williams
	27	2/7	Lectured at Corps School Poperinghe (Sanitation). Lectured on water supply at Corps School. In the afternoon investigated	J.T.Williams
	28	3/7	Examined control grounds Troops at Canal Bank, Hagebruck. Lecturing at 2nd Army School of Sanitation.	

J.T. Williams Capt R.A.M.C.
O.C. 77th Sanitary Section
38th (Welsh) Division.

Vol. 16

140/2043

Mar. 1917

CONFIDENTIAL.

WAR DIARY of

Captain D. Llewelyn Williams, R.A.M.C.,

O.C. 77TH SANITARY SECTION.

38th WELSH DIVISION.

FROM 1/3/17   TO 3/3/17

(VOLUME 16)

COMMITTEE FOR THE MEDICAL HISTORY OF THE WAR
Date 11 MAY. 1917

77th SANITARY SECTION — No. ORIGINAL — 38th (WELSH) DIVISION

Army Form C. 2118.

WAR DIARY
or
INTELLIGENCE SUMMARY.
(Erase heading not required.)

Instructions regarding War Diaries and Intelligence Summaries are contained in F. S. Regs., Part II. and the Staff Manual respectively. Title pages will be prepared in manuscript.

Place	Date	Hour	Summary of Events and Information	Remarks and references to Appendices
PESELHOEK	1	3/17	Inspection of camps in back area. Pay Parade. Investigation of Typhoid case in 10th Welch.	J.L. Williams
	2	3/17	Inspection of Divisional School & camps with Cmdg. Commander R.E. Officer. Attended a meeting re. Draft Water treatment at 17 C.A. Pumping.	J.L. Williams
	3	3/17	Inspection of D and E camps in the morning & in the afternoon investigated cases of D.A.H & Paratyphi in the 13/R.W.F. and proceeded to the 14th R.W.F.	J.L. Williams
	4	3/17	Special report to A.D.M.S. re Q on the remarks made by the Commr. S. when he visited the Divisional School at J Camp.	J.L. Williams
	5	3/17	Inspection of P.R.E. camp at Headquarters. Lecture to Corps School & also attended a conference of Sanitary Officers at D.D.M.S. York Corps.	J.L. Williams
	6	3/17	Lecture (Water Supply) Corps School. Inspected a Cress Ground at H Camp.	J.L. Williams
	7	3/17	Lectures at 2nd Army School of Sanitation. Huyebroek.	J.L. Williams
	8	3/17	Inspection of D.D.S. Camps. Two men of section sent to report as Inmates at K. Camp. Inspect of Shraadingh Chateau Ground in the afternoon.	J.L. Williams
	9	3/17	Inspected the whole of Canal Bank & was accompanied by the D.A.D.M.S.	J.L. Williams

Army Form C. 2118.

WAR DIARY
or
INTELLIGENCE SUMMARY.
(Erase heading not required.)

Place	Date	Hour	Summary of Events and Information	Remarks and references to Appendices
PESELHOEK	10	3/17	S.M. Corps. He found the ventilation of the Tunnel Dug-out defective & reported on this effect to A.D.M.S. of the 38th Division.	S.T. Williams
	11	3/17	Inspected Incinerator in Divisional Area since arrangement to remedy the defective ones. Weekly sanitary route report sent to the A.D.M.S.	S.T. Williams
		3/17	Church Parade. Cleaning up Camp. Drill with Gas Respirators.	S.T. Williams
	12	3/17	Arranging for sanitary equipment from R.E. Yard. Inspection of N. Group.	S.T. Williams
	13	3/17	Lecturing on Sanitation at Corps School, Poperinghe. Lecturing on "Water Supply" at Corps School. Investigation of an outbreak of German Measles in the Kings Liverpool Regt Rosen.	S.T. Williams
	14	3/17	Sam Section fixing a Spray Bath at Drying Rooms Poperinghe. Visited the Divisional School.	S.T. Williams
	15	3/17	Visited Canal Bank & inspected Field Sanitary arrangement with Lieut. Banks.	S.T. Williams
	16	3/17	Visited & inspected (with Lieut. Knapp, Adjutant CDS) all the baths & laundries	S.T. Williams
	17	3/17	of Division & made a combined report suggesting several improvements. Tried the cover of the Steam Supplying order to the Laundry & mess up a sleeve for the purification of the water.	S.T. Williams

T2131. Wt. W708—776. 500000. 4/15. Sir J. C. & S.

Army Form C. 2118.

WAR DIARY
or
INTELLIGENCE SUMMARY.
(Erase heading not required.)

Instructions regarding War Diaries and Intelligence Summaries are contained in F.S. Regs., Part II. and the Staff Manual respectively. Title pages will be prepared in manuscript.

Place	Date	Hour	Summary of Events and Information	Remarks and references to Appendices
PESELHOEK			5th Corps. We found the ventilation of the Tunnel Dug-out defective & reported on this defect to A.D.M.S. of the 38th Division.	S.L. Williams
	10	3/17	Inspected Latrines in Divisional Rest Camp & made arrangements to remedy the defective ones.	S.L. Williams
	11	3/17	Weekly Sanitary reports reports sent to the A.D.M.S.	S.L. Williams
	12	3/17	Church Parade. Cleaning up Camp. Drill with Gas Respirators.	S.L. Williams
		3/17	Arranging for Sanitary equipment from R.E. Yard. Inspection of 3 Corps	S.L. Williams
	13	3/17	Lecturing on Sanitation at Corps School, Peselhoek. Lecturing on "Water Supply" at Corps School. Investigation & Inspection of 115th Brigade Transport lines & report to A.D.M.S. Investigation of an outbreak of German Measles on The King's Liverpool Rgt at Rosen	S.L. Williams
	14	3/17	Jam Lecturing & trying a Spray Bath at Drying Rooms Rasmus Peperingh. Visited the Divisional School	S.L. Williams
	15	3/17	Visited Canal Bank & inspected Billets - Sanitary arrangements with Lieut Banks	S.L. Williams
	16	3/17	Visited & inspected (with Lieut Nugee Adjutant C.R.E.) all the baths, Laundries & Division & made a combined report suggesting several improvements	S.L. Williams
	17	3/17	Found the cause of the Steam Supplying order to the Laundry & drew up a scheme for the purification of the water.	S.L. Williams

WAR DIARY or INTELLIGENCE SUMMARY

Army Form C. 2118.

Place	Date	Hour	Summary of Events and Information	Remarks and references to Appendices
PESELHOEK	18	3/17	Inspection of Divisional School. San Section cleaning its camp. Gas Drill.	Lt Williams
	19	3/17	Inspection of the 114th Brigade Transport Lines which were found in good order. Lecturing at Corps School Poperinghe on "Field Sanitation"	Lt Williams
	20	3/17	Lecturing at " " on "Water Supplies". In the afternoon inspection of Divisional Troops Camps. Inspected Cart horse Laundry & drew up a scheme for filtering the dirty water before discharge into a ditch.	Lt Williams
	21	3/17	Analysing various waters taken at the Lab. also testing the amount of available chlorine in various samples of Chlorinated Lime. Inspection of the transport lines of the Machine Gun Coy of the 113, 114, & the 115th Brigades.	Lt Williams
	22	3/17	Visited the Belgian Army & inspected the Baths & Laundries of the Belgians at La Panne.	Lt Williams
	23	3/17	Latrines & Urinals sent to I. Camp. Inspection of the sections of the D.H.C. Found the Sanitary arrangements very good.	Lt Williams
	24	3/17	Routine work. Visit of O.C. San Sect. of the 55th Division, showed him round some camps. Sanitary reports sent to A.D.M.S.	Lt Williams
	25	3/17	Church Parade. Investigating method of poultry ing wash at Chateau Lovie. Paid 131 Field Ambulance.	Lt Williams

Army Form C. 2118.

WAR DIARY
or
INTELLIGENCE SUMMARY.
(Erase heading not required.)

Instructions regarding War Diaries and Intelligence Summaries are contained in F. S. Regs., Part II. and the Staff Manual respectively. Title pages will be prepared in manuscript.

Place	Date	Hour	Summary of Events and Information	Remarks and references to Appendices
PESELHOER	26	3/17	Inspection of the cooking & sanitary arrangements of the section of the D.A.C. The ADMS who was present was very satisfied. Lectured on "Sanitation" at VIII Corps School Poperinghe.	Lt. Williams
"	27	3/17	Lectured on "Water Supply" at VIII Corps School. Visited the Battalion at HOOK C.C.S. Inspected the following camps in the afternoon. Zorn Farm, Numbers from Hospital Farm.	Lt. Williams
"	28	3/17	Submitted plans for remodelling A.14 Latrines to A.A. & Q.M.G. Supply demolition of old Latrine & P. Pits (disused) was accompanied by him through the A.Q. staff.	Lt. Williams
"	29	3/17	Inspection of P. Pits (continued) & further report & recommendation sent to A.A. & Q.M.G. through the ADMS. Inspection of the Sanitary arrangements of the units located in Dickebusch Ruins. The ADMS made recommendations & idea as to be carried out.	Lt. Williams
"	30	3/17	Inspect of H & X Camps & made General Suggestions to O.C. as to improvement.	Lt. Williams
"	31	3/17	Inspection & routine work of Sanitary Section. Weekly reports sent to the ADMS.	Lt. Williams

D. Newlyn-Williams Capt. R.A.M.C.
O.C. 77th Sanitary Section
31/3/17

CONFIDENTIAL.

WAR DIARY of

Captain D. Llewelyn Williams, R.A.M.C.,

O.C. 77TH SANITARY SECTION.

38th WELSH DIVISION.

(VOLUME 17)

FROM 1/4/17 TO 30/4/17

COMMITTEE FOR THE
MEDICAL HISTORY OF THE WAR

Date = 6 JUN. 1917

Army Form C. 2118.

WAR DIARY
or
INTELLIGENCE SUMMARY.
(Erase heading not required.)

Instructions regarding War Diaries and Intelligence Summaries are contained in F. S. Regs., Part II. and the Staff Manual respectively. Title pages will be prepared in manuscript.

Place	Date	Hour	Summary of Events and Information	Remarks and references to Appendices
PESELHOEK	1	4/7	Analysing sample of water from Boesinghe & Villagewoods. Chem. analysis shews presence of nitrite but no acid gas in ice in McCulkey Brit. Sroes for Cooking purposes. Inspection of water carts of the Div. Ammn. Column	S. L. Williams
"	2	4/7	Sanitary Section erecting an incinerator in Elverdinghe Chateau Grounds. Lecturing instructing Sanitation at 8th Corps School.	S. L. Williams
"	3	4/7	Lecturing on water supply at Corps School. In the afternoon Inspected the Wye Thie Camp & gave instructions to a water trouble to a water machine gun coy. which arrived from England. Shop of P camp which was found satisfactory. Found the Canteen at Church Hut unsatisfactory – gave instructions and a warning	S. L. Williams
"	4	4/7	Inspection of Elverdinghe Chateau Grounds. Lectured & demonstrated the water carts at Canal Bank & Elveringhe Chateau to R.M. Officers	S. L. Williams
"	5	4/7	Lectured in the both East at Chateau drew to the 8th Corps Headquarters. Investigated Contacts of Typhoid (Par) Co. C. Quiad Honingle at Canal Bank	W. L. Williams
"	6	4/7	Visited 114th Brig. H.Q. & arranged as to location & erection Frosl. shed at D camp. & I Camp. Lectured Inspected the Camp. of the 38th Signal Camp. also I Camp. Lectured in the evening at Divisional School on Sanitation.	S. L. Williams

Army Form C. 2118.

WAR DIARY
or
INTELLIGENCE SUMMARY.
(Erase heading not required.)

Instructions regarding War Diaries and Intelligence Summaries are contained in F.S. Regs., Part II. and the Staff Manual respectively. Title pages will be prepared in manuscript.

Place	Date	Hour	Summary of Events and Information	Remarks and references to Appendices
PESELHOEK	7	4/17	Inspecting Tunnel in Canal Bank. Found ventilation & cleanliness improved. Inspected of Ovalyphus cases in 19th (HLI). Examined the contacts. Weekly san'y ret'ns report sent to found.	R.Williams
	8	4/17	Church Parade at 9 am. Inspection of Mortar's Camp with O.C. (Mach Gun Sect & Adjutant R.P. Made several suggestions for improvements. Lecture & Demonstration on Water Cart at 3 Coys of 7 Bn Williams to R.W.R. 114th Brigade.	R.Williams
	9	4/17	Lecture & Sanitary Demonstration to the Officers & men of the 114th Brig. Mach gun Company at S. camp. Conference of O.C. Sanitary Sections of the 2nd Army at S.M.S. Office Hazebrouck. Sanitary Sections taken from Divisions & made Corps Sections. These units will in future be Army troops but attached to D.M.S (Corps). The 77th Sanitary Section takes over our No 1. Had include Ypres. (2 Divisions in our rest area -- the 38th & 55th)	R.Williams
	10	4/17	Conference of the three Sanitary Officers in 59th Corp with D.M.S at his Office at Cont-Hire. Sanitary Inspection of Canthose Laundry & Farm.	R.Williams
	11	4/17	Left my Office at 8 am. Picked up the O.C. San Sect of 115th SK Division & visited & inspected Ypres & the Camps along the Ypres Road etc.	R.Williams
	12	4/17	Visited the camps. H.Q. 2 ffi. 55th Division also the R.D.M.S in the evening. Visited the M.S.K 13 Brigade Transport.	R.Williams

T2134. Wt. W708-776. 500000. 4/15. Sir J. C. & S.

Army Form C. 2118.

WAR DIARY
or
INTELLIGENCE SUMMARY.
(Erase heading not required.)

Place	Date	Hour	Summary of Events and Information	Remarks and references to Appendices
PESELHOEK	13		Visited Canal Bank. Found it satisfactory. Demonstrated water cart to Brig Genl Atkinson of 55th Corps & Vieille Ypres & inspected water supply at Oosthoeve	
	14		Leaving for England (on leave)	

Army Form C. 2118.

WAR DIARY
or
INTELLIGENCE SUMMARY.
(Erase heading not required.)

Instructions regarding War Diaries and Intelligence Summaries are contained in F.S. Regs., Part II. and the Staff Manual respectively. Title pages will be prepared in manuscript.

Place	Date	Hour	Summary of Events and Information	Remarks and references to Appendices
RESEMPRTERS	14/7/17		Assumed duties of acting C.O. 77 San Recrs. during Capt Phil Witherow absence	
			Inspected 55th D.A.C. L'Brit: School: Also A/Batt 276 & B/Batt	
	15/7/17		275 R.F.A. Ran Camps: Don & E (A/30 Central 28) in the afternoon	
			Inspected Indian Waggon Lines 275 Bde R.F.A. and A/275 Waggon Lines	
			also B/112 R.F.A. & No 3 Coy 38th Divl Train	
do	16/7/17		Made following inspections:– Offices area, Canal Bank, Reigersburg	
			Château and Elverdinghe.	
do	17/7/17		Inspected 234 Coy R.E., No 3 Sectn 55th K.D. Coy, & "C" Camp, & 55 &	
			56 Tn Brinch. Lectured to 113 Inf. Bde Trans Officers at	
			Water Cart at 2 p.m. and to 38th Divl Lecture at 5.30 p.m	
do	18/7/17		Visited Machine Gun Farm, Elverdinghe, Camps B, C, D,	
			and E. Also No 151 Coy R.E. at Ardren Farm	
do	19/7/17		Saw D.D.V.S. Visited 131 Fd Amb, Rinwood Farm Hospital in morning. Afternoon	
			in mornings also 113 Inf. Bde Ramparts Afternoon	
			–Kary Farm,	
do	20/7/17		Inspected F, G, and H Camps. Officers Mess. Returned Water Carts & 27th	
			Dinschüt. I Lunch at 5.30 pm Told men relieved from Offices at circuit	

Army Form C. 2118.

WAR DIARY
or
INTELLIGENCE SUMMARY.
(Erase heading not required.)

Place	Date	Hour	Summary of Events and Information	Remarks and references to Appendices
PESELHOEK	21/4/17		Inspected Camps D and E, also 55th F.R.Q. C.R.E.	
do.	23/4/17		Visited Ypres, Canal Bank, Ferry Farm, Blue Farm and Elverdinghe Chateau. Called at 130 Field Ambulance.	
do.	24/4/17		Office work at Headquarters. Visited D.H.Q., Stenge Farm, B Camp.	
do.	25/4/17		Inspected Hd.qrs 276 Bde R.F.A., Signal Coy R.E. 35th Divn and No. 1 Section 35th D.A.C. Visited some Etrennels reported as bad. Also visited W Camp. and also	
do.	26/4/17		Inspected Sections 1, 2, 3 and Hd. 119 B.A.C. of the 35th D.A.C. Visited Russel Farm, A/30 central Depot and D Camp. Capt. O.H. Williams returns from leave	

Followay made
Capt. R.J. I.C.
for O.C. 77 Div Train

Army Form C. 2118.

WAR DIARY
or
INTELLIGENCE SUMMARY.
(Erase heading not required.)

Place	Date	Hour	Summary of Events and Information	Remarks and references to Appendices
BISSELHOEK	26	4/17	Arrived back in camp from leave about 10.30 p.m.	Lt. Wesley Williams
"	27	4/17	Office work in the morning — reading of orders & making up back-work. Visited D.C. camps and arranged for fortnight of athletic work with Staff Capt. of 114th Brigade. Arranged for the renewing and light of Clayton Disinfecting Chamber.	Lt. Williams
"	28	4/17	Visited all the baths and laundries in No 1 Sanitary Div. for special inspect. with the exception of Cent. here Laundry — all were satisfactory	Lt. Williams
"	29	4/17	Church Parade. Visited S.A.C. & recommended methods of burning manure. Inspect. units along Steenvoorde Road.	Lt. Williams
"	30	4/17	Visited Canal & inspected located debts with teeth Sands R&we c regt. Secko with Capt. Worrock, Sanitary officer respecting of 39th & 39th Division.	Lt. Williams

L. Wesley Williams
Capt. R.A.M.C.
O.C. 77th Sans Section.

May 1st. 1917.

www.ingramcontent.com/pod-product-compliance
Lightning Source LLC
Chambersburg PA
CBHW081550160426
43191CB00011B/1885